PUNK ROCK Etiquette

The Ultimate How-to Guide for Punk, Underground,
DIY, and Indie Bands

Travis Nichols

Roaring Brook Press
New York

Text and Illustrations copyright © 2008 by Travis Nichols

Flash Point is an imprint of Roaring Brook Press,
a division of Holtzbrinck Publishing Holdings Limited Partnership
175 Fifth Avenue, New York, New York 10010

Library of Congress Cataloging-in-Publication Data: Nichols, Travis.
Punkrocketiquette:theultimatehow-toguideforpunk,underground,DIY,andindiebands
/ Travis Nichols.—1st ed.   p. cm.
ISBN-13: 978-1-59643-415-8   ISBN-10: 1-59643-415-5
1. Rock music—Vocational guidance. I. Title.
ML3795.N53 2008
781.66023—dc22
2008011706

Roaring Brook Press books are available for special promotions and
premiums. For details contact: Director of Special Markets, Holtzbrinck
Publishers.

First Edition September 2008
Cover design by Danica Novgorodoff
Book design by Lissi Erwin
Printed in the United States of America
1 3 5 7 9 10 8 6 4 2

To my wonderful, supportive mom for teaching me to jump on the bed.

To Jessica for the UN-FLIPPING-WAVERING encouragement and motivation.

CONTENTS

INTRODUCTION

So, you fancy yourself a rock and roller. Some kind of big shot. Because you've got it. You've got the music INSIDE you, and it's burning to get out. You can feel it. It's going to happen.

How lucky for you to be alive in days like these—it's never been easier to get a band together and get out there and DESTROY all on your own. In the dark days of music, musicians were at the mercy of the industry, pining for attention and a chance to "cut a record," as they used to say. Nowadays, any pack of hoodlums can record and put out their own music, have a badass Web site and superpro-looking marketing crap, and book shows and tours all over the world. So get to it! Huzzah!

That said, it's never been harder. Because EVERYBODY is doing it. Open any subculture rock zine and you'll find fifty bands you haven't heard of and fifty new releases you're supposed to buy. And each of the fuhskrillion indie bands out there . . . has a badass Web site and superpro-looking marketing crap. Or at least, you know, a MySpace page.

As time passes, punk dies, is reborn, and dies again. Bands come and go. Musicians get older and disillusioned and stop being involved, content to whittle on their front porches and perfect the art of brewing sun tea. Gradually, the wisdom of the ancients is forgotten.

Although reinvention is crucial, there are some timeless truths that must be preserved!

That's where this book comes in. Playing in a band is pretty much the raddest thing a person can do. Anyone with the inclination should go for it, and this guide is here to help you along the way. Yes, just as Shamu teaches Shamu Jr. her tricks, punk rock etiquette must be passed down to the next generation. And this book isn't just for the new kids. We could all use a little etiquette refresher now and then.

But don't think it's an attempt at establishing RULES. Do what you want, baby! That's what it's all about.

Let's get started.

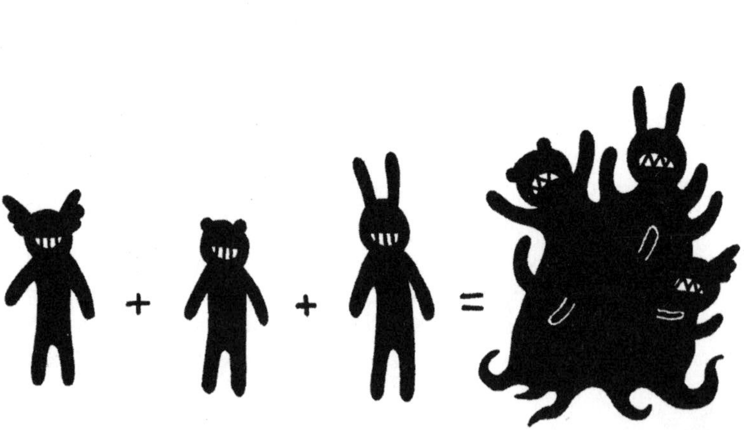

FORMING A BAND

Who you should or shouldn't have in your band depends on your goals. If you're just planning on screwing around in the garage a couple of times a month, it doesn't matter so much. However, if you plan on playing shows at all, it starts to get a little trickier. If you're wanting to put out records, tour, and maybe get on any sort of label, this crap is important!

Posse Up!

So how do you hook up with your fellow jongleurs? Well, most people just round up some of their lousy friends and get to it. Many great bands started out when a group of pals with no experience or skills decided to pick up instruments and learn as they went. That is the ESSENCE of DIY, baby! But a lot of the time, stepping out of your inner circle is necessary if you want to be any good.

Lots of folks post and read listings online seeking bandmates, which works, but if you're going to shows and are actively involved in your scene, you should meet plenty of people who want to get a band together. Here are some types of potential bandmates and the pros and cons of each:

The Tortured Poet: This kid *hurts*. He/she has a raggedy notebook full of lyrics that are probably about being sad or in love or both. You might have to stop him/her from cutting little thumbholes in his/her long-sleeved shirts or putting candles onstage.

> **Pros:** Comes loaded with ideas, chicks/dudes dig him/her.

> **Cons:** Hates compromise of "vision," chicks/dudes find him/her cheesy (yeah, it can go either way).

The Guitar/Drum/Other Hero: Also known as "the Shredder," this potential bandmate can PLAY, son!

> **Pros:** Skills, skills.

> **Cons:** Long solos, likely arrogant.

The Rock Star: Eager, rowdy, and flamboyant, this so-and-so is living the dream—groupies, money, power. Wants the white-towel treatment. A throwback from the arena rock crap that punk rock rebelled against, yet . . . kind of rad.

> **Pros:** Can be fun to be around, good stage presence, good clothes.

> **Cons:** Potentially a total prick, likely a drunk or druggie, wears sunglasses indoors (and not in an ironic way).

The Techie: Is your amp broken or on the fritz? Motion for the Techie. You'll be wailing again in no time. Armed with one of those all-in-one tools, he/she will take care of your gear. It's good to have one of these people around.

> **Pros:** Fixes stuff.

> **Cons:** Has too much crap, be it drum stuff or guitar pedals.

The Rich Kid: Their parents would prefer to raise doctors or lawyers, but Rich Kids want to ROCK. The Rich Kid has the hookup for gear the rest of the band can't afford, and can sometimes even supply a van! It ain't all roses, though.

> **Pros:** They … have money. And maybe even a pool.

> **Cons:** Parents make them miss shows for college prep courses and job interviews with friends from "the club."

The Poor Kid: Poverty is about as punk as it gets. Poor Kids give a band cred, and they're usually REALLY into music. That guitar/drum kit/keyboard/banjo is their baby. Music is their outlet to express their animosity toward the upper class (and if they're so inclined, possibly their ticket to BEING in the upper class—dost thine hypocrisy know no bounds?!).

> **Pros:** Scene points galore, passion.

> **Cons:** Has trouble getting off work for shows. Tour? Good luck. Unless he/she quits his/her job for it … and then you'll have to spot him/her cash along the way.

The Delinquent: Everyone loves a criminal. Robin Hood and Billy the Kid—those guys were KICKASS. But if your band's Delinquent dabbles in anything violent or something that could get YOU in trouble, steer clear.

Pros: Cred, keeps you stocked in guitar picks and snacks.

Cons: Probation officer meetings get in the way of practicing and touring.

The Whatever: This guy/girl just wants to play. No big whoop. Doesn't really add or subtract from the equation. Most often a bass player. 'Nuff said.

Pros: Up for whatever, doesn't argue.

Cons: About as exciting as a sack of doorknobs.

Most common combos: Of COURSE there's overlap. Don't get all pissy. Here are the most frequent combinations.

Tortured Poet/Rock Star: Usually a "front man." God, what a dorky term. If it's a guy, he probably wears eyeliner.

Tortured Poet/Poor Kid: Parents just don't understand. This might just be *the* most common potential bandmate combo.

Guitar Hero/Poor Kid: Ah, the bedroom shredder. Hours and hours of solitude and noodling around have produced this, this beast of rock and roll. All hail. And give her some of your fries.

Rock Star/Delinquent: All too common. This bastard will steal money from a bartender's tip jar because he/she doesn't think the band was paid enough. Motel-trashing trouble.

Guitar Hero/Techie: Subscriber of various gear magazines. Don't let him grow a goatee and you'll be okay.

Poor Kid/Delinquent: At the risk of sounding like somebody's grandpa, these people are hoodlums. These kids are all right.

Rich Kid/Delinquent: Happens sooooo often. An attempt to regain lost scene points.

The Look

Appearances are pretty important. People will judge you. *Sssshhh.* Yes. I know. That's not what music should be about. But in this day and age, with a fuhskrillion bands clamoring for attention . . . you just . . . just THINK about it.

Before you take your band public, you need to spend some time on this. How you look is going to send a message to the audience, so make sure it's a message you WANT to send.

If you go to hundreds of shows, you'll get pretty good at knowing if you're going to like a band or not by looking at them as they set up. Here are some examples of what to expect by employing a smidge of prejudice:

If the band you're about to hear has **dirty clothes that don't fit and crummy equipment**, they're going to be awesome. Unless they're college kids trying to look all DIY. Then they're probably crappy.

 If everyone in the band you're about to hear is **skinny and dressed in black T-shirts and tight jeans—except for the drummer**, who is wearing baggy shorts, a colored T-shirt (read: not black), and flip-flops—get ready to hear a BADASS drummer. Yeah, there's a reason these guys signed this guy on. He honed his skills by listening to crappy music like Dave Matthews Band and 311 and became a technical HERO because of it. The guys in the band are pretty hung up on image and seek to change their drummer bit by bit, and if the band lasts more than a year, he will become indistinguishable from the rest of them (unless they compromise and let him keep his soul patch). Also, this is probably a Christian band.

 If anyone in the band you're about to see is **wearing one of their own T-shirts**, leave. Now.

 If you see **guys that look like the dudes that played saxophone in your high school marching band** (you know, newsies hats and khakis), ESPECIALLY if you see them setting up a laptop, this band is going to be boring.

If you see **Mohawks and plaid pants** . . . well, that's obvious.

 If everyone is wearing **tucked-in button-up shirts, nice pants, skirts or dresses**, and somebody (likely the guitar player who doesn't sing) is wearing **Ray-Ban sunglasses**, well, do you like college music? Pop!

 If the band consists of **eastern-European-looking** men and/or (especially) women with **choppy haircuts**, you're going to hear some weird singing. And some handclaps.

 If you see **four or five guys** setting up . . . and there are **nine or more wristbands between them** . . . and each of them has some **crazy screen-printed shirt** with the illegible name of whatever band . . . and one or two of them has **tattoo sleeves and lip rings**, yeah, you've heard this band a thousand times with a thousand different names. If that's your thing, lucky you. One more CD in the pile. One more mass e-mail you'll get every week. Every. Single. Week.

 If you're about to see a band, and they're a bunch of **fat dudes with beards**, prepare to be DESTROYED. Awesomely.

So remember the old adage: *Always* judge a book by its cover. You don't have to be the coolest bunch of guys and gals, but consider putting a little effort into it. If someone in your band absolutely insists on playing shows in their crummy workout clothes, you might have a problem. Or maybe, just maybe, you could ALL dress in workout clothes. Make it your thing.

Costumes or rad outfits can take a band to the next level. An already great band could don gold masks and capes and suddenly become completely flipping amazing. Again, playing music should be about the MUSIC, but playing live brings a visual element that should not be overlooked.

The Name

Okay, listen up. Your band's name is crucial. You're going to be stuck with this thing. Don't be hasty. Here are some Do's and Don'ts.

DO	DON'T
Pick something that sounds like your band. or be ironic.	Use wordplay. That's for clowns.
Go online and search **EXTENSIVELY** to see if the name is taken.	Mizspell wordz in yur band's name. That's for doucherock.
Say it out loud. Look at it written.	**MISSPELL WORDS IN YOUR BAND'S NAME. SERIOUSLY.**
Let your choice settle for a few days before you commit to it.	Use weird capitalization in the name. SeE hoW laMe iT LoOkS?
Choose something that is obviously pronounced.	

Other ideas: Consider obscure historical figures, childhood references (be careful!), old books and films, flipping through a dictionary and slapping your finger down a few times. Yeah, that's a little bit middle school, but at least four of the bands you listen to did it that way whether or not they would ever admit it.

How to Secure Your Spot in the Band

So you're in a band you really like. This is IT. Your meteoric rise to the top is totally impending. So how can you make sure that you won't, nay, CAN'T get kicked out of the group? Well, if it's not "your" band, you've got to do as many of the following as possible to make sure that getting rid of you isn't an option.

- ☐ Date the lead singer (this could backfire if the relationship ends)
- ☐ Own the van
- ☐ Be, like, amazing at your instrument(s)
- ☐ Own the majority of the equipment
- ☐ Provide the practice space
- ☐ Book the shows
- ☐ Be the offspring of a celebrity/industry-type
- ☐ Be nice

Practicing

One of the toughest things to do as a band is get together to practice consistently. The more people you have in your band, the more schedules you have to deal with. If you've got a member who can't seem to ever get to practice or acts really annoyed to be there, maybe he or she shouldn't be in the band. If you're trying to play shows and tour, you want to be with people who are dedicated and have the time for it.

Practice as much as you can without getting sick of it. When you're practicing, work on your songs, yes, but when you're getting ready for shows, practice your whole set. You've got to be in good rockshape to get through all of your songs without running out of steam. If you move around a lot onstage, don't practice sitting down. Stand up and do what you do live. Dance, baby, dance. Do some jump kicks. Spin your guitar around. YEAH! You might feel silly doing that when it's just your band in your practice space, but if you sit and watch your hands while you practice and then get onstage and suddenly try to flip out while playing, you'll embarrass yourself.

A good practice space is vital. You have to be concerned about volume, security, and availability. If you've got a garage or big room you can use at home, awesome. Put blankets and mattresses up to block the sound. Your neighbors still might complain, however, and then you'll have to figure something else out. Some bands rent storage units or share a rehearsal space with other bands. If you go that route, make sure it's secure and at least moderately climate controlled. Otherwise, see if someone in the band has a backroom at work you can use.

It would be ideal to have a place where you can safely leave your stuff. That way, you don't have to spend precious time setting everything up and taking everything apart every time. Show up, rock, then go about your business.

SONGS AND RECORDING

The last thing this book would ever delve into is telling you how to write a song. Relax. It should be said, however, that bands break up over writing all the time. If there's more than one hotshot songwriter in a band, things could get hectic. Some bands have one writer who brings his or her gifts from heaven to practice and teaches the rest of the band what to play. Some bands have a more collaborative approach where everyone writes their own parts. Do your best to secure the songwriting arrangement early on. Otherwise, when your bass player wants to sing the lame song he wrote and put it on your record, you've got two choices: You can suffer through it and embarrass yourselves, or you can shoot him down and create a rift in your band.

Here, pals, are some of the options you have for recording those oh-so-inspired, kickass songs. The options range from lo-fi gutter style . . . to total balla (shot calla). What used to cost thousands of dollars can now be done for a fraction of the cost. But don't mistake this information for claims of authority or supreme knowledge. There are many books on recording. This is just to give a taste. Just a little taste.

Four-Track

Dirt cheap and lo-fi chic. Every time recording technology advances, used four track recorders get cheaper. Less advanced models can sometimes be found online with a microphone and all necessary cables for less than fifty bucks (plus shipping), and after that, your main investment will be cassettes.

Your basic four track will allow you to record one or two tracks (or parts) at a time and build up to four. If you have two microphones, you can track a vocal and guitar part at the same time if your four-track record allows for two tracks recording at the same time. More advanced models let you bounce multiple tracks onto a single track, thus increasing how many parts you can record. Many a great record was recorded in a bedroom on a four track (or even on a single-track, cheapo tape deck) with a ten-dollar microphone. On the other hand, many a crappy, unlistenable record was recorded in a bedroom on a four track with a ten-dollar microphone. There's good lo-fi, and there's baaaad lo-fi. Just because your recording is free of high-dollar pretension doesn't mean it has to sound like it was taped via payphone outside a convenience store. Unless that's what you're going for.

Four-track recorders are pretty easy to figure out. When all needed tracks are laid down and you have the volume levels where you want them, you can go from the outputs onto a cassette deck and make copies that way, or you can hook up to a computer and make digital files that can be put on CDs or sent to a record-duplication facility.

Digital Four- (or Eight- or Sixteen-, etc.) Track

Many of the limitations of four-track cassette recorders are eliminated when you step up to a digital recorder. Many have built-in effects such as reverb, chorus, flanger (use sparingly!), echo, delay, etc., so you can save a pantload on pedals and cables (however, your live show and recorded stuff should sound similar, so you'll probably want to be able to re-create those effects). Increased sound quality is another bonus.

Computer

There are lots of free programs for recording on your home computer. There are also programs that cost loads of money. Macs come with GarageBand, which beats the pants off an old four-track. It's definitely not as advanced as the high-end programs out there, but who do you think you are, anyway? A computer can be a one-stop studio—recording, mixing, duplication. You can buy a mixing board and other external equipment, or use the internal stuff included in most decent software.

With all of the DIY recording options, you'll need a decent microphone or two. You can get one that will do the job for the cost of a couple of records or a hoodie. No big whoop. If your singer makes a lot of hard PPP! sounds, have him or her back away a little bit. You can also make your own pop filter by bending a wire hanger into a loop and stretching pantyhose over it. Then attach it with the ends of the wires so the filter is a few inches away from the microphone.

You'll also need a good place to record. If you're recording at home, try out different rooms for the most desired sound. You might find that drums sound best in your bedroom, guitar sounds best in the kitchen, etc. A common go-to for vocal recording is the bathroom due to the reverb-y quality. Experiment.

So . . . in what order should you record everything? Drums, if you have them, should usually be tracked first. Your drummer can listen to a guitar or bass playing along in headphones so he or she will know where they are in the song. When you have the drums tracked, record everything else in whatever order makes sense to you, probably with vocals last. It's easier to sing along to music than to play along to singing. But do what you want!

Studio

Using an actual studio has many benefits. Better equipment and people who know how to use it is one. A professional studio's sound will trump your garage's. If it doesn't, you're in a crummy studio. Studios charge by the hour, by the song, or by the day. There might simply be a session charge.

If you're going to use a studio, there are a few things you should do before you get there. First and foremost, have your songs down. Don't use studio time to write songs. You're not Def Leppard. You could spend TEN YEARS in the studio and you could never top *Hysteria*. Don't even try it, amateurs.

Michael Mayer ran a studio in Lubbock, Texas, for several years, which is in no small part responsible for the bitter (yet lovable), balding curmudgeon that he has become.

Michael, for the sake of his studio engineer comrades across the globe, agreed to compile a list of DO's and DON'Ts about recording. It quickly became a list of pet peeves. Attempts to keep him calm and on track with cinnamon candy and soda became more and more difficult, and this is what he was able to dictate before he derailed into an unrelated tangent.

Tune your instruments. Seriously. There's nothing "punk rock" about being out of tune. It just makes you sound like you don't know any better. Fool us all into thinking you're moderately capable and buy a tuner.

Drummers: I've got a mind-blower for you. Those heads? The ones that have been on your kit since you bought it off Craigslist? You know, the ones that are brown (but used to be white)? Those need to be changed before you record. Change them about one or two practices before you record.

Guitarists and bass players: new strings, kiddos.

Practice. A lot. Go over the songs you plan on recording. Work out beginnings and endings. You should all be able to play through the song without hearing any vocals. Get a metronome and figure out the tempos. You might even let your drummer listen to the metronome through headphones while you practice so he's not dragging those fills and rushing those awesome blast-beats.

If you're paying by the hour, the studio is not the place to work on arrangements, unless you have an unlimited budget. If so, then by all means.

Long story short, get your crap together BEFORE you show up. If you need to borrow someone's amp to record with, be familiar with it BEFORE you get there. If you want to add some awesome three-part harmony on that chorus, figure the parts out BEFORE you show up.

Drummers: I need to have another word with you. That kit you have, with the rototoms, the China, and the 14 other cymbals, auxiliary percussion, and the "cage" that it all bolts to? That crap's gotta go. You can barely play in time as it is. Adding more to the mix is NOT helping.

Here's what you should have: a rack tom, a floor tom, a kick, a snare, hi-hats, a crash, and a ride. That's it. When you learn to play THAT kit rock-solid, then we'll talk about you getting a "splash" cymbal or some other ridiculous thing you think you need.

Guitarists: I can't make your crappy Peavey Bandit sound like a Marshall stack. Save your paper-route money and buy a Marshall. And no, that emulator-pod-thing you have doesn't sound like a Marshall, either. Neither does the Marshall pedal that you have between your crappy guitar and crappy amp.

Be willing to take criticism. I'm assuming that you have some amount of trust in the person you're paying to record your band. Listen to them. They have done this a LOT. If you disagree with something they offer creatively, fine. But don't get butt-hurt if the engineer points out that you're rushing/dragging/sucking.

Leave your ego at the door. I'm looking at you, lead singer.

Record yourself before you go to the studio. Even if it's just on a crummy boom-box. Lots of bands have NO idea how bad they are.

I've seen recording break up more than one band.

Be realistic about what you want out of your recording. Budget accordingly.

Leave your friends/girlfriends/boy-friends/hangers-on at HOME. They will do nothing but distract you and get in the way. This will cost you time and money and ultimately hurt the project.

If you have someone record you for free, you'll probably get what you pay for.

PUTTING OUT YOUR MUSIC

So you've recorded your masterwork. It's so flipping good. Surely the landscape of music will be changed forever. But first you gotta put the sucker out. There are many options.

Something to Hold

Your first thought might be CDs. Sure, why not? If you want to get them pressed professionally, expect to spend about a thousand bucks for a thousand CDs. You might find a better deal if you look. If you're a new band just starting out, you might want to avoid laying down fat cash for a thousand CDs. Let's get real for a second. Come sit over here.

I don't mean this in a cruel way. You're great. I really cherish you . . . but chances are, your new band will break up before you sell even half of those CDs. So . . . well, maybe you should start off a little smaller. For now! And then we'll see? Cool? Okay, great. I'm so glad we can be so open together.

Now that that's settled, there's nothing wrong with CDRs. You can make them at home much cheaper and in smaller numbers. And you have more control. Cases can be bought in bulk, or you can make your own sleeves out of cardboard. Give the planet a hug by raiding thrift stores, free bins, and your own collection for CD cases. Sleeves and inserts can be printed on copy machines or home printers. If you want to save the planet, there are companies that print CD and record sleeves with vegetable inks on 100% postconsumer recycled paper. You can also make your own sleeves out of the cardboard from cereal boxes and screen print them. Handmade stuff that obviously took effort appeals to the people.

HOW TO MAKE CD sleeves out of cereal boxes

ÜBER BRAN

1. eat
2. draw/measure
3. cut
4. print / draw / stamp on blank side
5. fold
6. glue flaps
7. stack under heavy books
8. remove, test
9. insert CD, liner notes

Screaming and Violence

THANKS.

Vinyl isn't dead! If you think it is, just look to your friendly neighborhood DJs. They (and the underground music scene from punk to hip-hop) are keeping it alive. Vinyl LPs and 7- and 10-inch records can be manufactured pretty affordably. Just like with CD manufacturing, the more you have made, the more cost effective they are. Do some browsing online for a good deal. And again, most places can also make the sleeves/inserts, or you can provide them yourself.

Cassette tapes! Hooray! Make one! Tape culture lives! There are dozens of cassette-only labels out there. And you know what they say: Every time someone utters the phrase, "I don't have a tape player," an angel loses her *Garbage Pail Kids* collection. What happened to mix tapes, people? Oh . . . mix CDs? Not. The. Same. Thing. Anyway, tapes are rad. You should make one. And you should own a tape deck.

Columbus, Ohio's, The Kyle Sowashes (completely amazing, by the way) have a cassingle they put out by recording over existing cassingles, which they thrifted, covering the existing sleeve with a sleeve of their own. Other bands have done this, too (before and since), and it's a great idea. Hit the thrift stores and stock up, for a whopping twenty-five cents a piece in some places. Just scotch tape over the little holes on top so you can record over *Color Me Badd* or whatever, and then record dead air after your music until the end of the tape (or not). Draw/paint over the original cassette writing, cover the original sleeve with your own or make a new sleeve from card stock or cardboard, and you've got yourself a cassingle. And you saved some plastic from the landfill. *Gasp!* You really DO care! Whatever format(s) you choose for releasing your music, just take a little time and put in some effort. DIY doesn't have to mean sloppy and cheap-looking. It should mean, "HEY! I don't need big money to do something wonderful. I'm capable and awesome!" You'll be happier with a better product, and so will the people who are paying for your music.

Artwork/Sleeve/Liner Notes

We, as a people, like pretty things. We judge music by its album art. Think about it. When you go to a bookstore or record store, you first pick up things that catch your eye. Food companies spend millions on making their products look good. Cartoon characters hold up giant bowls of cereal in mid-milky-splash. So put some thought into your liner notes. If no one in the band is artsy-fartsy, find a friend to do it.

Be creative. Try to come up with something completely new and awesome, or riff on a classic standby. Album art themes that will be done over and over until the end of time include silhouetted birds and trees, blurry kitchen photographs, the band sitting solemnly on a couch or standing in a field, a sad and/or kissing couple, and anything with an old-timey nautical theme.

There's also some technical garbage that needs to go in the liner notes of the CD. Obviously, you'll need to include the name of the band and release, as well as a track listing. Your Web address is important. You might want to include the names of band members and what each member plays. It's also nice to thank anyone who has helped you out along the way. Put a copyright notice in there. The correct format is "Copyright (date) by (name of band or song writer)." You can also use

back of cd case

rasslin • hit the mats!

1 choke hold my heart 2 tapped out
3 half nelson, half portuguese 4 pin
5 no cup! 6 singlet and ready to minglet

all songs © 2008 by rasslin. all rights reserved. you've been warned.
unlicensed duplication causes chronic jock itch. punkrocketiquette.com

the © symbol. (Look at some other albums for examples.) This isn't absolutely necessary, as most things are copyright protected once they're put down on paper (or plastic). It just serves as a warning to the pirates out yonder. Actually registering a copyright through the U.S. Copyright Office is voluntary. If you reeeeeeally want to do it, it's not hard. Check out www.copyright.gov. Everything will be on public record, your ducks will be in a row, and you can finally get a good night's sleep, you paranoid worrywart! And speaking of copyright, band names canNOT be copyrighted.

Performing Rights Organizations

Feel free to skim riiiight past this section. This stuff might suck the punk spirit right out of you. But "performing rights organizations" should be mentioned. Whether or not you want to register with BMI or ASCAP, etc., is up to you. The role of a performing rights organization is to enforce copyright, to license, and to collect money on your behalf for the use of your music in any sort of public performance (such as on a jukebox or at a restaurant). If you look at your music collection, you'll see that even some of the more indie stuff has performing rights information in the liner notes.

Unless you're big-time, you most likely won't see a penny in royalties. But it could come in handy if you write a funny holiday song and mainstream radio stations across the country start playing it. Also, you might get a check for a few bucks ten years after your band breaks up because a song of yours was played at a WNBA game or something. It's weird, but it could happen!

If you're not on a label at all, you'll probably want as much airplay as you can get to sell your music, and if you're registered, it's your right to allow stations to play your stuff without payment. Some stations might be übercautious and want a letter granting royalty-free permission. What a world.

Your Web Site

Fellow space cadets, welcome to the future. The age of flying cars! And cities built on clouds! And pizza in pill form! And—wait. Aren't we supposed to have flying cars by now? I was promised flying cars! At any rate, what we DO have is the Interwebs.

Part of what has made it so hard for an indie band to be heard these days is the Internet. It is just too easy to have a Web site and music available for online listening and downloading. So easy that everybody is doing it. So we're all drowning in an ocean of . . . each other.

Your band's Web site is one of your most valuable tools. It will help in promoting shows and even booking them. You can blog about your adventures and show the world how good-looking you are with pictures and videos. There are many ways to go about building a Web site, and here are some of them, in order of easiest/cheapest to most complicated/expensive.

Social Networking, Portal, and Profile Sites
They're free, they're easy, they're not superprofessional. You have an account, your sketchy uncle has an account, your friend's dog has an account, every restaurant and bar and store in the world has an

account. And they're flooded with ads. But you can stream songs and post pictures and shows, and many even have a feature for selling your music online. If you plan on releasing music and touring and making a real go of it, you should have more than a MySpace account. That said, they make good supplements to a regular Web site and are good for networking.

Freebie Web Sites

If you don't want to spend any money on your Web site but still want one that stands alone, there are several free hosts out there. Just do a search for "free Web site" and have your pick. Many come with templates for easy editing if you don't know how to use HTML. What else do they come with? Ads. But if you can live with that, this is your best option.

Freebie-ish

The biggest expense of a Web site is hosting. You can grab domain names for around eight to fourteen bucks a year, but hosting can cost you about that much a month. There are places to find free hosting if you look, but you'll most likely be stuck with a long domain name with a bunch of backslashes and junk. However, you can use URL (domain name) forwarding to link your domain to a free host. In other words, register your desired domain name, and then go to a freebie hosting site and get an account. Check with the site where you registered your domain, and look up "domain name forwarding." Expect to pay a few bucks a year for the service. Enter in the address of your freebie site, and you're golden. Then, when your mega-fans type in your Web address (the domain name you registered), they'll be taken to whatever free-hosted address your domain forwards to. That way, they won't have to type in the crazy long address from a free provider to get to your site.

For the Reals

Search for a host that also registers domains and you'll be set. It's not very expensive, especially if you have a band fund or split it between members. It's worth it if you want to appear professional and not be exposed as the pack of ne'er-do-wells that you are.

You'll have to learn how to code in HTML or another webby language. It's not tough. There are tons of tutorials online, and you can also steal bits of code from other pages.

So What Should Go on My Band's Site?

For the love of all things holy, do not flood your Web site with animated pictures and slideshows. The average viewer would sooner close a browser window than wait two minutes for your page to load. Make sure you include a band bio and information about each member. Put in some photos and some streaming videos if you have them. Have a couple of songs available for free download, so the kids can have something to hold on to. And, of course, there should be a page listing upcoming shows. You might want to list them on the front page, so viewers won't miss them.

Selling Your Music Online

In the old days, if a band wanted to sell their CDs/records/tapes/merch other than at shows, they'd set up a mail order "business." They would take out ads in punk rock magazines and tell interested parties to send well-concealed cash to an address, and they'd mail out the music in return. This is still done today, of course, but mostly within the zine culture. It's still totally viable to do it this way, and it's punk as hell, but you should probably take it to the next step by selling your releases through your Web site.

You can still accept cash by mail to sell your stuff, but now anybody can set up an online store to take online currency and credit card payments. There are several easy-to-use options including PayPal and Yahoo! Shopping Cart. They take small fees from each transaction but make buying and selling a breeze. It takes that extra step out of the process, for the buyer who might not feel like making a trip to the post office to drop off cash or a money order. And here's a secret: people don't consider their online balances to be real money! They're not physically holding the cash, and that makes it easier to spend—just like a credit card. Suckers.

When the MP3 was born and began to spread, record labels started to flip out. As people bought fewer CDs and records (though isn't it nice to actually HOLD the music in your hands?), the industry scrambled to find a way to make money from online music. The result? They can still squeeze blood from the rock via the iTunes store and other online music retailers. The great news is that small labels and independent musicians can use the same resources and get their music heard (and purchased) by a worldwide audience.

But before you sign up with a service to sell audio files online, read the contracts thoroughly. Find out how much you will make per download after all fees are taken out. Is it worth it? Or should you stick with mailing out physical recordings?

MERCH

Ah, *merch*. See, "merch" is short for "merchandise." It's, like, a cool abbreviation. Merch is for promotion and making a little cash, and it's really important. You don't want people to go home empty-handed, do you? Some people think that the music should speak for itself and putting out a bunch of junk is a waste of time, energy, money, and resources. Perhaps they're half-right. But isn't STUFF just great?

After CDs/records/tapes, which should come before anything else, the most common forms of band merch are shirts, buttons, and stickers. You can have your shirts made for you, or you can easily do them yourself on a beautiful, sunny day when you'd rather stay indoors (sunlight is SO 1998). Buttons are fun and cheap, and so are stickers. Most merch can be made affordably, and it's a good way to promote your band as well as make some gas money on the road.

How to Screen Print Your Own Shirts and Patches

Photo-Emulsion Method

There are a few ways to screen print. The photo-emulsion method is most common, and it's really easy once you get the hang of it. It's a little daunting at first, but just go for it. In the simplest of terms, here's how it works:

First, you need a design. Draw it on paper in opaque black ink. Don't get confused about positive and negative images. Just draw it as if you're going to be printing black ink on white T-shirts. Just remember that what you draw will be what gets inked. If you're new to screen printing, stick with a one-color design. When you're more comfortable and want to try out two or more colors, go for it. You'll need a separate screen for each color, and therefore a separate black ink drawing to begin with for each layer of color.

Next, you might want to get a kit at a hobby or art-supply store. You can score one for about fifty bucks. They come with emulsion, drawing fluid, emulsion remover, a screen, a squeegee, and ink. Most kits come with either fabric or acrylic ink. If you're making shirts, make sure you get fabric ink. If you can't find a kit, or if you can't find one that suits you, get all of the stuff separately. You'll probably want colors that don't come with kits anyway, since they usually have just red, yellow, black, and blue.

You'll also need the following:

- ☐ shirts or whatever you're screening on
- ☐ a clean work area with plenty of space
- ☐ a tabletop or hard surface to screen on
- ☐ a dark room such as a closet or cupboard
- ☐ a lamp with a clear (incandescent) 150-watt lightbulb (or something to power the bulb and let it hang)
- ☐ something to scoop ink (like a spoon)
- ☐ a damp towel to wipe up stray ink
- ☐ masking tape
- ☐ a piece of cardboard
- ☐ a nearby copy shop
- ☐ a snack
- ☐ a piece of glass large enough to cover your design (optional)
- ☐ a small fan (optional)
- ☐ a big sheet of black or dark paper (optional)

1. Spoon some emulsion onto your screen and spread it evenly and smoothly with your squeegee so it coats both sides. A thin layer works best. Also, don't worry about putting emulsion all the way to the edges of the screen. Just put on as much as you need for your design. You can put masking tape on the rest after your screen is burned and ready to print. This saves emulsion, which ain't cheap, people. Once you've spread on the ol' emulsion, put it in a dark room to dry. Having a little fan blowing on it speeds it up a lot.

2. Tell your roommate (you know, the one who always leaves the back door unlocked) to stay out of your dark room, and head to your friendly neighborhood copy shop with your design. Make a high-contrast (just black, no grays) transparency of what you want. Some people like to use two transparencies taped together so it's nice and opaque.

3. Your screen may or may not be dry when you get home. It's okay to give it a little touch—just make sure it's dry before you move on. Then it's time to burn the screen. This will also take place in your little dark room. If you've got a big sheet of black paper, place it on the ground where you are going to burn your screen, to help fight evil light leaks. Lay your screen flat-side down. Place your transparency on it with a piece of glass on top so it is sure to be flat, flat, flat up against the screen. Taping it down also works, if you don't have tiny lines.

4.

Hang your lightbulb a foot or so over your screen. Most sources tell you to use a clear (incandescent) 150-watt bulb. You can also get away with using a regular 100-watt bulb, and it should work fine. Anyway, shine that thang at your screen for about an hour and fifteen minutes. Don't be alarmed that the room is kinda bright—it doesn't matter as long as the light is close and beaming straight down on your design/screen and there aren't other light sources.

5.

Have a snack.

6.

When time is up, take all the stuff off your screen. You should faintly see your design. What was covered by the black on the transparency will appear a little lighter than the part where light was free to hit. The emulsion that was exposed to light has baked on, and the emulsion that was blocked by the black on the transparency will wash away. With cool water (preferably with a little pressure), wash the screen until the unbaked emulsion is all gone. Now the ink will be able to go through the screen where there is no emulsion. So yeah. There's your stencil. Set it outside to dry.

7. When your screen is dry, use masking tape to cover the non emulsioned edges on the nonflat side. Also, if part of your design came off when you were washing your screen, you can use a paintbrush and a little drawing fluid to fill it back in. NOW you're about ready to print.

8. When screening a shirt, put a piece of cardboard inside it so the ink doesn't go through both layers of cloth. Set the shirt down on your tabletop and smooth out any wrinkles. Spoon some ink on the screen (the nonflat side so that the flat side can lay against the shirt) in a nice line outside of your design. Put the screen on the shirt and squeegee the ink across the screen. This is another part you'll have to play around with. Some people make one pass with the squeegee, and others make a few. It all depends on the pressure you exert and how much ink you use. Trial and error. You can test things out on fabric scraps until you get it figured out.

9. As you screen things, set them out or hang them up. Just make sure they don't touch each other. Fabric screen-printing ink takes a long time to dry on its own, and it will get everywhere if you're not careful. If you want to switch ink colors, you'll probably want to wash the existing ink off your screen first. Don't worry. It won't wreck the screen. If you're doing a multicolored design, wait awhile before putting a screen down on top of an area you've already screened.

10.

When you've screened everything, and it's all dry enough that it doesn't come off when you touch it, you have to heat-set the ink. Otherwise, the shirts will get wrecked when washed. The last thing you want is to let the kids down, right? Right! This is the part you should be really meticulous about. Iron each shirt (with a piece of fabric on top so it's not directly touching the iron) for thirty seconds on both sides (inside and out). When you're done with that, put the shirts in the dryer on high heat for, seriously, like an hour. Burn those fossil fuels, baby. Ride your bike instead of driving for a few days to offset your crime against the environment. If you don't drive, oh, take cold showers for a while. There.

11.

When the dryer buzzes and you reeeeeally feel like the ink is totally set, you're done. Get those walking billboards out there. And do not, repeat, do NOT wear your own band's shirt. *Seriously.*

Multicolored Designs

For designs with two (or more) colors that need to line up properly, just make some registration marks where the second screen needs to go, either by using masking tape or pencil marks (this is much easier to do on patches or posters). To ease that strain, come up with a design that doesn't HAVE to be exact.

Non Emulsion Method

If you want to go the easy route, and you have a design without any teeny lines, you can make a screen for printing without the hassle of burning and waiting and dark rooming and water blasting. You can use a printout or drawing of your design and trace it onto the screen with a pencil and then paint the design with modge podge and let it dry. Then you can skip right to step 8.

Where to Score Shirts for Printing

T-shirts can be purchased wholesale online, and if you're not a jerk, you'll get them from a sweatshop-free company. If you're super rad, you'll buy shirts made from organic, sustainably produced cotton. Another way to get Earth-and-people-friendly shirts on the cheap is to buy them secondhand from thrift stores. You can go for the blank shirts, or you can even buy nonblank shirts and just screen them inside out. It's two shirts in one! Go for a wide assortment. And get some hoodies if you can. The kids sure love their hoodies. The only small hassle with going the thrift store route is that it takes longer for people to pick them out at the merch table because every shirt is different. Every shirt is different?! Holy crap. If that's not punk rock, I don't know what is.

Screen Printing Posters, CD Sleeves, Etc.

To screen print fancy show posters or super-special sleeves for your releases, use the same method as above, but use acrylic screen-printing ink. Also, you don't have to heat-set them. Just let them dry completely and you're good to go.

Buttons/Pins

One-inch buttons. A punk standard. Three-inch buttons? No! This isn't a Sunday school fund-raiser. Although . . . I could see 3-inchers working for some bands. Like, for those headbands-and-legwarmers synthy pop bands. Yeah, that would be pretty rad. Otherwise, go for the 1-inch.

Someone in your town probably has a button maker, or you can find someone online to make them for you. Twenty to twenty-five bucks for a hundred is the standard these days. If you want to make them yourself and make them for other bands and projects and make some rollin' cash, button makers aren't all that expensive. Slap down $200 to $300 online for the Model 100 (recommended for quality and durability), and you can pay it off pretty quickly (especially if you make buttons for other people). Piece of cake. Make sure you buy one that comes with a circle punch or you'll regret it. Most people who sell the machines include parts for one thousand buttons.

The size of the circle of paper that will become a 1-inch button is 1.313 inches (part of it rolls down the sides). You can fit forty-two of them on a piece of 8.5 x 11-inch paper. Keep your design simple (these things are tiny), and keep your file at 150 or 300 dpi and print them with a laser printer for quality's sake. You can put your band's Web site and a little message around the lip of the button if you position it right.

So, do you sell the buttons or give them away? That's your call. Anything from free to fifty cents works. Even a dollar sometimes. Or try "donations welcome" and see how that goes. If you made them yourself, they cost you about four cents apiece to make, you bum.

Vinyl Stickers

Ah, just do an online search for "vinyl stickers" or "band vinyl stickers." Upload your art, blah blah blah. Does EVERYTHING have to be explained? Does baby need a wubbie? Wait. That was harsh. You're wonderful. But please, don't put your stickers all over town. *Please.*

Other Merch

There's all sorts of silly crap you can get with your band's name on it. Koozies, playing cards, key chains, guitar picks, pens. Crap like that. You should probably stay away from that sort of thing. However, a foam finger would be pretty funny for a peppy powerpop group. For metal or hardcore bands reeeeeally going for the "we drink a lot" thing, sheesh, just get some custom coasters and get it over with.

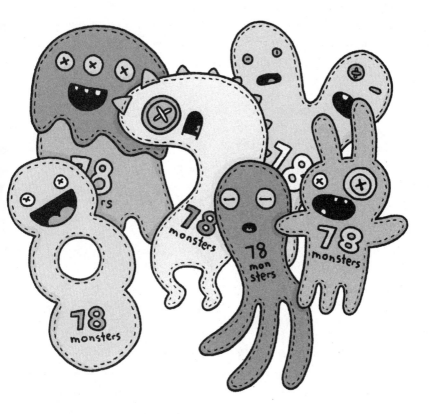

STAGE ETIQUETTE

When you've got your set down in practice and you're ready to take it public, you'll need to secure your grand entrance. If you don't have prior experience, getting those first few shows can be a little daunting. Take the pressure off by playing at a party or house show. If you're involved in your local scene, you'll know where the bands play and who to talk to about booking a show. You might have to hand over a demo CD or e-mail a Web link if you don't know the promoter or venue operator personally. Even the biggest, most competitive cities have venues that are great for bands that are just starting out. Again, the best way to get shows is to be involved. Go to shows!

Once you've booked a show, you gotta know how to behave on stage. The desire to address stage etiquette was the genesis of this book. It is so very important and so often overlooked. Performing isn't just about getting up and shredding through your songs. Whether you're playing in the living room of the local punk house, the corner stage of a sketchy bar, or in some huge, tacky amphitheater, the same principles apply. And it's separated into three parts: *the Setup*, *the Thunder*, and *the Departure*.

The Setup

Most of what is crucial about the Setup and the Departure is that THERE ARE OTHER BANDS ON THE BILL. Before you step onstage, you should have as much stuff together as you can. Drummers should have drums and cymbals already attached to stands. Guitarists with pedal boards should have all of their little buddies plugged in to each other. If preamps can go on top of amps safely before lifting/rolling them onstage, that would be nice. The goal here is speed! The sooner you set up, the sooner you rock, the sooner you get that fat cash.

Oh, the sound guy: If you are playing somewhere with a real PA, there's probably going to be some dude working the mixer. Be nice to this person. Introduce yourself before the show. They'll ask you what kind of setup you have. Good information early on will make for a quicker and smoother sound check. And during sound check, TRY not to be so particular when it comes to your monitors. If you can't hear your drummer's low tom in your bass player's monitor, can you just be okay with that? Thanks! Every room is going to sound different, so just get it close and nobody will know any different. You'll be fine.

Be good at tuning. Quickly.

Have a set list prepared that everyone can see. Few things are more lame than band members asking each other what they should play next while onstage.

You should also know how long of a set you're supposed to play. If you're supposed to play for 20 minutes, play for 20 minutes. If you're supposed to play for 40 minutes, play for 40 minutes. If you're supposed to play for three hours, you're playing at a fratty/blue-collar sports bar, and you had better know some typical rock-and-roll covers. Oh, man, what did you get yourselves into? Please note that your set time might include your setup and takedown. Just another reason to get on- and offstage wicked fast.

The Thunder

That's right, titans of rock! It's time to shake the pillars of Mount Olympus. You are incredible. You are unstoppable. So . . . just play the songs, right? Well, yeah, sure. But there are a few other things you should probably do as well. And if you have trouble remembering the following things, make little notes of them within your set list.

Things to do during the set:

1. Thank the venue operators/residents for having you, and thank the other bands.

2. Mention your merch/mailing list.

3. If you're strangers in a strange land, don't be afraid to mention you're looking for a place to stay if you haven't already made arrangements. More on that later.

4. Do what yo' momma taught you—be nice to your audience. Nice bands that kind of suck can get pretty far in life.

5. At the end, tell people to "stick around for _____" (name of next band). That's a cool thing to do.

Things NOT to do during the set:

1. Yell at fellow bandmates about how they're screwing up. Control, baby. Control.

2. Talk smack about the venue or sound guy or, well, ANYBODY.

3. Damage equipment that's not yours. Screw up your own crap as much as you want, if that's your thing. But if you're going to trash your guitar during the last song, try not to make it so obvious that you've switched to your crappy, beat-up Strat rip-off for your little tantrum. Yeah, people saw you!

4. Offer free breast exams after the show. I don't care if you're being ironic. That's skanky.

5. Play longer than you're supposed to. It's better to play less. Leave 'em wanting more, warriors.

The Departure

In short, get the hell off the stage. Now. Grab your stuff and BOUNCE. Do not put your guitars in their cases. Do not disassemble your drums. Do not, repeat, do NOT wind up your guitar cables onstage. This is the most common display of bad stage etiquette known to rock and roll. It is arguably the most amateur move a band can make. And I've seen some "big" bands violate this suggestion, this rule, this MANDATE.

The bottom line is: When you're out of the way, the next band can set up and there won't be a lull in the show. Lulls make people get bored and leave. That doesn't necessarily affect you if you already played, but if everyone exhibited proper stage etiquette, the underground music scene would be a better place. Look out for your fellow jongleurs.

When you haul ass to get off the stage, you can fan out, delegate the duties, and fully maximize the spoils of the magic you just dispensed upon the crowd. Someone can get to the merch table while wallets are still burning. Someone can organize all of the equipment into a good area (not a four-person job). Someone can flirt/schmooze and get free drinks/food for the band. GOD, you kids are rad.

When the show is over, if there is *door* money to be had, someone may need to ask for it. Don't be shy. Sometimes you HAVE to ask for it, or, well, you won't get it. Slimeballs. Go up to the guy taking door money or the venue operator and say something like, "Thanks so much for letting us play!" Then wait for a response having to do with getting you paid. If that doesn't happen, say something like, "So how'd we do on the door?"

When you get paid, tip the sound guy (if there was one) a few bucks. It's customary. Five is nice. But don't screw yourselves. Also, if you're playing in your hometown and there are touring bands on the bill, give them your money. Seriously. Splitting twenty or forty bucks among your band members will get *you* a late-night snack, but it could get some travelers to the next town. Which brings us to ...

The Role of the Local Band

If you're playing a show in your town with one or more touring bands, you're there for support. Touring bands that aren't well known get the shaft from opening local bands every single night in the world of underground music. The lousy brats bring their friends to the show

(good!), rock out for them (good!), and then most of said friends leave right after (bad!). So, basically, people are paying to see a local band. Unless the venue operator pays the local bands (some folks don't understand that locals just shouldn't be paid when there are touring bands on the bill), the travelers are still paid, so it's no big deal.

Even so, if you're playing locally, do what you can to keep your pals around for the touring band(s). Promote the show as theirs. Not yours. Tell everybody how rad these people are. Offer to make a nomad sandwich (see "Headlining" box) at the show. Unfortunately, you can do only so much to keep people around for touring bands. If they don't want to listen to something new, they're lame anyway. I mean . . . what are they there for? To hang out in the parking lot and throw sticks at stuff? Wow, the people in your town are terrible.

Oftentimes, a traveling band can hook you up with a show in their town if and when you go on tour. Or they can at least tell you who to talk to. But don't expect them to help you out if you practice bad stage etiquette. Wind those cables offstage; watch, cheer, and dance for the other bands; and if the venue operators simplemindedly gave you any door money, give it to the people on the road. They need it much more than you.

HEADLINING

The term "headlining" should be completely stricken from the indie rock vernacular. Period. In the arena-rock world, the band who plays last is the "headliner." The one with the biggest lettering on the marquee. The überstars.

For bigger shows with well-known bands in the indie scene, the big-name draw usually plays last. There's little chance that people will leave before their favorite hotshot band plays. However, for lesser-known or unknown bands, it might be best for a local "opening" band to actually play after the touring band or bands. Ideally, a local band before and after touring bands is tops. This is called a nomad sandwich. So if you're a local band playing after a touring band, don't call it headlining. That's embarrassing.

GAS MONEY

a tour journal of REVEL IN THIS

LET'S MEET THE BAND

Alright, so Vern and I had booked a short tour to test things out. Revel in This had never been out for more than a weekend, so we gathered our contacts from previous bands and set out to set Texas on FIRE. You know, with music.   Metaphor.

I got to the rendezvous point (Quinten's house) and met up with the team. We loaded everything perfectly into Vern's mom's minivan.

This is the thing we're best at.

We booked the first couple of shows with our friends, A Grin and a Grenade. And, of course, they were late.

You jerks wanna go on tour?!

CARAVAN, HO!!

The drive from Lubbock to Amarillo was uneventful.

We got to the venue, a rad old ballroom where Johnny Cash, Roy Orbison, Jerry Lee Lewis, Elvis, and all those guys played back in the day.

James Brown was arrested for lewdness here.

COOL!

People started arriving and hanging around, so we set up. The opening band had to cancel, so it was just A Grin and a Grenade and us.

Man, we were super sloppy.

♪

We got paid pretty well and sold a fair amount of merch. Add that to a decent-sized band fund, and spirits were high.

We are... incredible.

After a good night's sleep, we had breakfast with some friends.

Then it was off to Wichita Falls. YEEEAH!

Suddenly...

SLAP!!

It's a blowout!

No, the tread came off.

Vern and Quinten worked on changing the tire, and Ross (from A Grin and a Grenade) and I ran to where the tread was and took pictures with it. Because we're children.

So we drove the rest of the way on what looked like a freaking bicycle tire. What a crappy spare.

We finally made it, and it turned out that Alan (Grenade) got a speeding ticket on the way.

These... are bad omens.

And yeah... The show pretty much sucked.

I was nervous that night. What if the rest of the shows suck? What if WE suck?

In the morning, we said goodbye to A Grin and a Grenade as they headed back to Lubbock. As for us...

ONWARD!

We got the tire fixed, gassed up, and hit it!

In addition to selling a bunch of merch and making enough door money to pay for gas for the next couple of days, we got to stay at the venue for the night. Rad!

We had the place all to ourselves, and we stayed up way too late playing pool and watching the huge TV.

We woke up at 10 or so when a bible-study group started making snacks in the kitchen.

All of us... except Quinten.

So I gingerly coaxed him up.

Q! E!

We hung out for a while at some weird mall in the next (weird) town.

Smells.

I played a sweet video game where you move around to dodge bullets.

Our San Antonio show was another house show.

We arrived at a home full of high-schoolers playing video games and eating.

There was a big music room, and I played around on drums while a guy played metal riffs on a totally evil guitar.

We thought the show was going to be in there, so we started bringing stuff in.

But the show was in the back yard.

We rocked out as the sun set. The neighbor's dog never stopped barking.

The only weird thing was that the kids stood in a huddle about twenty feet away and stared at us.

But they liked us, I guess, because we sold tons of merch.

Afterwards, one of our hosts made us fruit cups!

We decided to head to San Angelo instead of staying the night. We wanted to stay at our friend Jeannette's place for two nights to have a day without travel.

Late that night, I got an email.....

hi! thanks for playing at our house. after you left we put on your cd and everybody was dancing!!!

So the next day, we got to Abilene early to try to figure it out.

I called a guy who runs a mini-golf place where my high school band used to play and he let us have the show there! Yes!

It was hard to get the word out again, but we had about 25 people there.

We stayed at my mom's house. Yeah, that's how frickin' punk we are.

I love you, mommy!

The next morning, we went back to Lubbock. And tour... was over.

So here we are. An indie band amidst a million indie bands. I'm ready for longer tours and bigger shows, and maybe that will happen. Money-wise, we broke even, and that is a success at this point. We'll see you on the road!

PREHEATING YOUR
OVEN OF DESTRUCTION

It's the ultimate. The open road. A new town and new faces every night. No masters, no curfews, no rules. "Wait," you ask as you pee on the side of a highway with a blanket of stars surrounding you, the breeze of a part of the country that until now you've only read about blowing through your hair. "We're getting PAID for this?"

Well, hopefully. The truth is, touring is ROUGH for an unknown band. Fortunately, the punk network is, for the most part, generous and supportive. At the very least, you'll always have some disgusting house to sleep in.

There's a lot to touring. It's not just hopping in the van and peeling out. It takes a lot of planning and preparation. Of course, you COULD just hop in the van and peel out. It happens, and it . . . sometimes sort of works. You'd be better off actually BOOKING and packing properly and ensuring that you're not going to end up broke and stranded in the middle of the desert (though you can prepare all you want and that still might happen).

A new band probably shouldn't jump right in to a month-long tour at first, even if you've been on long tours before with other bands. Your true colors shine through when you're away from home for a few days, and if you realize that you all hate each other with three weeks to go, you're screwed. The harsh reality is that most bands break up after their first tour. Play it safe and start small. Do a few one-offs and weekends and see how it goes. If it's still all kittens and rainbows, go for a couple of weeks—then a month! If it's still going well, quit your jobs, sell your possessions, and become rock nomads for life!

Booking

The thing about booking is that it . . . sucks. If you have a label rep or a friend with booking experience who can do it for you, you're set. If you're doing it yourself, get ready for headaches. Hey. You can do it. Just pick your route, and maybe a catalyst, such as one super-amazing show or event to book around. Maybe it's a killer hookup somewhere across the country that you KNOW will pay off big-time, or maybe it's a record release in your hometown on a certain date. Maybe there's a comic convention across the country you want to go to. Instead of flying there, why not have a week of shows toward the convention and then a week of shows on the way back? Once you have that one date figured out, map out your route and go from there. You'll want to start booking two or three months in advance, and know that you'll most likely still be working on it from the road. Yeah, it works like that.

Days off? Avoid them! A proper DIY tour shouldn't have a lot of planned days off. If you're driving an average of four hours a day, it's not an efficient and effective use of your time. Don't be a weenie. You came to rock, so ROCK. If you have a group of friends you want to spend time with, sure, take a breather. Just don't make a habit of it.

Splitting up the booking duties may or may not work for your band. To avoid confusion and overlap, only one or two people should be working on it. Keep all of your information in one place and keep it organized. You don't want to go scrambling for an important phone number you scrawled on a napkin when you're lost on the wrong side of the tracks in a strange city. You're endangering the band! Also, if you have a computer, keep numbers and addresses and other important information on file there as well.

When mapping out your route, try to eliminate long drives as much as possible. On the East Coast, rad towns are an hour apart sometimes, but out West, expect to do some five- or six- (or seven- or eight-) hour drives. Don't forget about the small towns! Some of the best shows you will ever play might be in cities with less than fifty thousand people. So many small towns have vibrant scenes where EVERYBODY goes to shows because, well, that's all there is to do. You can score serious bank and make some HUGE fans. Try being completely unknown and pulling fifty people in New York City, Boston, Austin, LA, or other places where there's too much to do. Good luck, Jack! Plus, playing small towns helps break up long drives.

The best way to book a show in a town is to have played and been received well there before. Of course, that doesn't help if it's your first time in that particular place. The second-best option is to have a hookup from another band you've played with before. This is why it pays to be nice! Show swapping can take care of a great deal of work. Hook up a band in your town and have them hook you up in theirs. Nothing beats calling in a bunch of favors at once. If you are fortunate enough to get a contact list from another band, exploit the HELL out of it. "Hey, ____. Our dear friends ____ told us to contact you about getting a show in ____." You get the idea.

When you've exhausted your direct hookups and you still have a bunch of holes in your schedule, it's time for the harder stuff. Look up venues and find their contact information. Some places have promoters or one person that they use for booking, and they're constantly swarmed with show requests. Be brief! Tell them who you are, what date you're looking for, and provide a direct link to your music online. Some promoters still want a physical CD or, *ugh*, a press kit. If you can avoid sending out stuff, avoid it. Save your money. It's not necessary in the age of the MP3. If you want to get booked somewhere that requires a press kit, that means a CD, a one-page bio, and a photo of the band. Be wary, pals. There are jerks out there just after free music.

Once in a while, you'll have an "opportunity" to play a show where you're supposed to presell tickets. This is called "pay to play", and it's HORRIBLE. And so not punk rock. Basically, this takes all of the promoter's, you know, *promoting* responsibilities and puts them on you. These shows are usually eight-bands-or-more showcases or battle of the band events. And you have to buy the tickets from the promoter, so if you don't sell enough, you're in the hole! This system is set up so a promoter/venue can be sure to get paid no matter what, and it doesn't benefit bands, no matter how they try to schmooze you with promises of cash prizes and quality networking. Bah. Promoters should promote, and musicians should musicate.

Loads of resources for booking your own tours can be found online. There are sites where people post their contact information and the types of shows they book. Just do a search for "DIY punk show help" (or something like that) with the name of the city you're looking to book. You might find a message board or an individual who can help you out, or you might find direct links to venues that you can contact. Sometimes you can find kids that regularly book shows at their local venues as a hobby. They do it because they're into music and they want cool shows to go to. Seek out these people.

When you make connections and you're finalizing shows, get all of the information you can: How many other bands there will be and who they are (knowing who the local bands are ahead of time and contact-ing them is a great way to ensure good promotion); how the money situation works (cut of the door or a guaranteed amount?); address and phone number of the venue and person booking the show, load-in time, the approximate time you'll be playing, etc. You may also want to get some extra info ahead of time, like where the good record stores (for gathering a few last-minute attendees) and places to eat are.

On tour, you'll have the opportunity to play at all sorts of places. Everyone has their favorites, depending on preference of intimacy, extra features, crowd, etc.

House Shows

Ah, the tradition continues. Rocking out in somebody's rumpus room, living room, or garage is FUN. These shows are often set up as parties or potlucks with an intimate crowd mostly made up of friends of the residents, so all inhibitions are thrown out the window—sometimes literally.

> **Upsides:** Video games, fooooood, often doubles as your place to sleep for the night.

> **Downsides:** Threat of cop shut-down, people still hanging around at 3 a.m. when you're trying to sleep before you have to get up early in the morning to make a long drive. And house shows are often at the local "punk house," which is usually really nasty.

Coffee Shops

Not just for hippie folksters and slam poets anymore! A lot of coffee shops have rock shows, sometimes in a backroom and sometimes right in the middle of everything. Melt the faces off the suckers who went there to study. Ha-ha!

> **Upsides:** Free drinks and bagels, mainline to the college and/or high school scene.

> **Downsides:** Rarely any door money collected, some coffee shops have volume restrictions.

Punk Hangouts

Every once in a while, some kids will get together and rent a warehouse, storage unit, or an old retail space in a crappy part of town. These types of places typically last about four months, so if you can get in during that window, you're golden. These places are fun and free-spirited.

Upsides: No rules, scene points like *woah, RAD*.

Downsides: No rules, crappy PA, dirty, danger of the place being shut down between when you booked the show and when you show up to play.

Youth Centers

If you can get a show at a youth center, ESPECIALLY a Christian youth center (watch those swear words), oh, wow, get ready for the white-towel treatment (literally). These places are run by grown-ups, and thus they're chockablock with arena-style hookups. You will be treated SO well. Be nice in return and you'll totally be set.

Upsides: Backstage area with deli trays, cold water, good money (even if you didn't make much at the door),

CLEAN place to stay (with a nice family or sometimes at the venue itself), big-screen TV, pool table, etc.

Downsides: Be on your best behavior, not the most punk rock place to play in the world . . . but who cares! They've got a HUGE TV.

Music . . . Venues

What is there to say? Some towns have actual music venues. They're often bars as well, but the main focus here is the ROCK. People go to these places because of bands, so . . . bring your A-game.

Upsides: It's an actual venue with door money and merch tables and a stage.

Downsides: Keep your eye on those venue operators and promoters. They can be a shifty bunch.

Bars

Sometimes this is your only option—the corner or stage of a stinky bar. If you work at it and go through good channels, you will have a good crowd and not a handful of renegade bikers who would love nothing more than to make a sissy-kebab out of your band with a pool cue.

Upsides: Drink tickets, drunk people spend money freely.

Downsides: Drunk idiots yell things.

In-stores

Cool record stores sometimes let bands play right there in the shop. It brings people in to (hopefully) buy records, and it puts bands in good context. Some stores do shows only in the afternoon, so you might be able to score two shows in a day.

Upsides: In-stores are cool.

Downsides: Most likely no door money taken, and what money you make . . . you'll be tempted to spend on music.

Other

There are all kinds of places for shows, so you might find yourself rocking out at any of the following:

- A furniture store after closing
- A park gazebo
- A decrepit concert hall
- A pedestrian bridge over a river in the middle of the night
- A high school cafeteria during lunch
- A beach, ankle-deep in the waves (ha-ha-ha, you beatnik)
- An art gallery
- A skate park

So, yeah! Book a tour and see where you end up!

Promoting

It's sad to say, but you can't really count on someone else to promote your shows well. You've got to do everything you can to ensure that you won't be playing to a big empty room. Worst-case scenario: At least the other bands will be there. Being around other bands is good for networking, but unless your van runs on friendship, you've got to get some paying future fans in there, too.

If you have fancy tour posters or flyers that you really want to use, ask the promoters or someone you know at each tour stop if you can mail them a few. This isn't necessary at all. A lot of scenes don't even flyer for shows anymore, and if they do, they can make their own, anyway. If you really want to, though, go for it. Tour posters should have your band's name, whatever fancy artwork you want, and your Web site address. Make sure there's a big blank space on the poster so information can be written in. A few posters will suffice for each town. One can go at the venue, and a couple can go at various points of indie rock interest, such as record and video stores. Don't waste 'em! If they're really nice, hold on to them and sell them at shows.

Here comes a road axiom: *The more you go, the more you know.* When you travel, you meet lots of great people. After a few tours, you'll have friends all over, which makes promoting a lot easier. Your friends have friends and contacts, and your shows, as well as your experience overall, will be better because of it. If you're a newbie, don't worry. You'll meet people along the way.

Try to meet people online ahead of time. Don't be a creep about it and spend two months hitting on people, and don't go around blanket spamming people in every city. Have a little self-control and strategy. Chat up a few people and get to know them. You know, like friends. Find out about cool stuff going on in town, etc. Make plans to hang out. You're more likely to get good promotion from far away if you show a genuine interest in people and LIVING, and not just in making sales.

If you actually ARE only interested in making sales . . . then just be a big phony.

Take it to the airwaves! Look up college stations in each city, and contact the promotions director via e-mail. Tell him or her who you are, a little about your band, and link to your Web site and music. Give him or her your show information and say that you'd be happy to send a CD to the station if he or she is interested. If you don't hear back in a couple of weeks, go ahead and call. If you leave a voice mail and still don't hear back, well, take a hint. Your next bet (and it might even work better) is to see if the station has a show that plays your type of music. Find out who the DJ is and send him or her an e-mail.

Your Chariot

A touring band needs a reliable conveyance. The most common way to get around on tour is by van. Your van is more than just your ride. It's your home away from home. You'll eat, sleep, pee in bottles, and LIVE in the thing for as long as you're on the road. Vans can get filthy pretty quickly. They can also break down on you. Not to mention, they're crazy expensive to get around in. Here are some tips to help ensure a nice trip.

Very Necessary

Have a mechanic you trust give your vehicle a thorough checkup to catch anything major before you leave. If you don't know a mechanic personally, ask around. There's a nice over-lap between the punk community and the . . . car community.

Keep some oil and premixed coolant (already has water in it) with you. You may need some car juice when you're miles away from a town. And even if you're in the middle of civilization when you need it, that stuff is expensive. So get it before you leave when you're still flush with cash.

 Don't leave your spare tire behind to make room for that extra cooler. Take the tire. Take. The tire. And a small jack and tire iron.

 Your registration and insurance should be current. You can go months and months without updating your registration and get a ticket only if you get pulled over, but if you let your insurance lapse and you get in a wreck, you're turbo-screwed.

Really . . . Consider This

Do you really NEED a giant van? If your band is a bearded five-piece with three full-stack amps and a double kick drum full-on metal kit, yeah, you do. And maybe a trailer. If your band is a lo-fi folky three-piece, you might consider a lovely sedan option. Many consider the station wagon to be the ULTIMATE touring vehicle, as station wagons have lots of storage space and get much better gas mileage than sixteen-passenger vans. Do a dry run with your loading. You might be surprised at how much you can fit into a small space. Tetris skills, baby. So if you can get away with it without sitting on top of each other, think about sizing down your ride.

Have a couple of reusable trash bags with you so your garbage doesn't end up all over the floor. Though, if you're like most people, it still will. You're gross.

If you're driving a big, dirty, sticker-covered van around the country, expect to be profiled by the law. And thieves. It's best not to advertise that you're a bunch of hooligans away from home and that you've got a bunch of expensive equipment with you. So keep that in mind before you put your band name and logo across the sides of your trailer. That's pretty lame, anyway. If you're going to have a bumper sticker, it should be church related or something family oriented, like a high school marching band sticker. Something that makes you look like honest, law-abiding citizens.

St. John's Elementary
Family. Community. Tetherball champs '06.

Take It to the Next Level

You know what's cheap now? In-car TVs. They can hang on the backs of the front seats or fit between them. I mean, it's no use to the driver or the person riding shotgun, but *they* have more important things to do. Think about it: You could be playing VIDEO GAMES. On the road. That's so balla. You're like Shaq or something.

If you have the means to acquire a reliable vehicle with a diesel engine, consider a conversion to greasel. It'll save loads on gas money. You'll just have to stop at restaurants along the way for their (free!) waste vegetable oils. All along the way, you will enjoy the sweet smell of french fries or tempura or doughnuts or whatever was cooked in the oil you're burning. Mmmmm-mmm!

And what if you went on tour . . . without a van or car? Bands have toured by train, bicycle, public bus, boxcar, boat, etc. You could do about two weeks of shows in the Northeast U.S. taking Chinatown Express buses alone. The U.S. is pretty much the only industrialized nation without a public train system you can really rely on, though, so if you want to go that route, you'll probably want to schedule off-days between each show. If you do go the public transportation route, you'll have to make sure you have rides to your venue/crash pad from the station in each town. Not all bands can pull something like this off. Double adventure!

Obtaining Your Tour Vehicle

If somebody in your band already has a van or car that will work for your tour, perfect—one less thing to worry about. If you don't have an in-band hookup, your next best option is to borrow Mommy's minivan. If Mommy already traded in the minivan for something small and sporty, and none of your friends have something you can borrow, somebody's going to have to pony up and buy something. If your band fund is pretty solid, you could go in on a van together, but be careful! Getting involved in owning something as a group is a big step. Are you guys ready for that? Perhaps it's best if somebody owns the vehicle you're using on his or her own.

Dude, Grab That Amp. And Get Me a Mineral Water.

So should you have a roadie? (*Note:* the term "tour support" is a million times more punk rock.) In the arena-rock world, road crews unload the trucks, carry the gear, set up amps, tune guitars, round up groupies, and basically do everything needed to ensure that the delicate geniuses don't pull a muscle or break a nail. In the underground music scene, you'll be carrying your own equipment, but it might be nice to have an extra pal around to work the merch table, help haul stuff, and change strings in a pinch. A good tour-support administrator will also shake down sketchy promoters for your cash. But SHOULD you have tour support? If you can answer yes to each of these questions, go for it!

- ☐ Can you stand being around this person for extended periods?
- ☐ Can they carry moderately heavy stuff?
- ☐ Do they bring the funny?
- ☐ Do you have room for one more person and their bag?
- ☐ Are they emotionally stable?
- ☐ Can they count?

Something else you should consider is how you'd handle the money situation regarding your tour support. If you have a daily food allowance, it would be nice to cut them in, so make sure that's something you can afford. They're taking time away from work and their regular life to help out some friends.

Okay, It's Getting Close . . .

Tour is a couple of weeks away. Make sure you have taken time off or quit your job and that your bills are paid while you're gone. You should confirm your shows two weeks before you're scheduled to play, so if your tour is long, you'll be doing that along the way as well. Double-check that the promoter or venue has your contact information in case anything happens on their end. Inevitably, however, something probably WILL happen without your hearing from someone. You'll show up where you're supposed to play only to find that the place is closed or double-booked, and you'll have to figure out something else. That's just the way it goes. And that's when having friends or acquaintances in town comes in handy. They might be able to throw together a last-minute house show or at least find you a place to stay.

Also, plan as much as you can for where you'll be staying in each town. Check with friends and friends of friends. You don't have to have it all down ahead of time. A lot of it will fall into place as you go along.

Print out maps and directions to each show and put them in your rockmobile right now, along with all of your venue and contact information. Before you forget.

Packing

Aw, just throw your junk in the van and go, go, GO! Or take some time to make sure you have everything you need. Your call.

Personal

How long is your tour? Do you tend to smell bad easily? These are questions you should ask when figuring out how much clothing to bring. Take what you'll need, but don't overdo it. There are other people to consider. Not to mention equipment. You know, *musical* equipment. For your *band* to play. On *tour*. So you probably don't need all four of those 3/4-sleeve blazers. Pack three. Wear the fourth.

If you're touring in the summer, pack lighter clothes, but still take at least a hoodie or sweatshirt. It can get chilly at night, even in Arizona. Likewise, in the colder months, pack some heavier clothes, but don't overdo it. You'll only be seeing people for a day, so don't worry about wearing the same thing several times.

If you don't want to be totally repellent, at least make sure you have enough underwear to last you. If you're going out for a month, you don't need thirty-one pairs of underwear, though. You'll most likely have an opportunity to do a load of laundry at some point. And if you go swimming in your underwear, that pair is totally clean. You'll

Two-Week Tour Packing Profile #1
THE MERCENARY

five black t-shirts

two red t-shirts

one hoodie

bandana!

one pair of shorts

two pairs of jeans

deodorant

camera or phone

lady stuff *

six undies

two bras *

toothbrush
toothpaste
bar of soap
(note: can be subbed for all-in-one liquid)

journal and pen or book

* depending on, well, you know.

four pairs of socks

one pair of shoes

also want to be set for socks in the same way. If you have superstinky feet, your van will smell like the inside of a shoe after three days of dirty socks. To solve this problem, pack a plastic bag to hold your dirty clothes. You can always toss a bunch of dirty socks and underwear in a sink with some soap and warm water, swish them around for a few minutes, and then dry them by hanging them out of a rolled-up window of your van or car while you drive.

Sometime before the tour, take a note of what bathroom stuff you use to get ready for the day and what you use before bed. Toothpaste, toothbrush, deodorant, cleaning stuff, etc. If you wear contacts, make sure you have your case and plenty of solution. Don't forget all of your creams, salves, balms, lotions, and ointments. You don't want to split in half onstage. Put all of that stuff in a toiletry kit of some kind. With the wear and tear of travel, plus the smooshing that goes on when things are piled, keeping the wet stuff together in a resealable plastic bag is a good idea. Major shampoo explosion!

Tour is probably not the time to come off your medication. Also, you might consider taking some multivitamins, since people tend to eat horribly on tour. If you take allergy medicine or pain medication from time to time, pack it up. In addition, someone on your team should have bandages, antibacterial stuff, and whatever light first-aid junk you might need.

You're not Elton John. You won't be flying to a show in your Concorde and then flying home with a two-day stopover in Monaco. You'll be sleeping on dirty floors and couches, and there won't be tiny mints on provided Egyptian linens. Every once in a while, you might score big and stay somewhere with spare beds, but you'll need to be ready for the times when that doesn't happen. You know, most of the time. Take a sleeping bag and pillow. If you're a total commando, a rolled-up hoodie makes a passable pillow.

You'll need stuff to do to idle away the hours of driving, not to mention the downtime at the venue before people start showing up.

Two-Week Tour Packing Profile #2
the (wo)man-at-arms

hat

eleven t-shirts,
assorted colors
and styles

camera

shades

music player

two shirts

three pairs
of jeans

phone

laptop

two pairs
of shorts

swimsuit

or

pack of socks,
one dozen pairs

one hoodie

one light jacket

four bras *

toothbrush + paste,
hairbrush, shampoo,
conditioner, soap
hair product,
deodorant,
face stuff,
shaving stuff

lady
stuff *

14 undies

journal, pens, books

two pairs
of shoes

* depending on what's happening "downtown"...

You'll be working a solid forty-five minutes a day, so take things to work on and do: books, zines, art stuff, video games, knitting, writing—stuff like that. One of the best and most rewarding time-fillers is documentation. Make a photolog or tour journal, and when you're old and gray, you'll be able to look back upon your rebellious, authority-spurning days with a sense of accomplishment.

Equipment

Do a dry run of everything you need to play. Each instrument, amp, pedal, cable. Don't forget those extra strings, picks, and cords. If you're going to be playing house shows or other nonvenue shows, take as many microphones and microphone stands as you'll need, since they probably won't be provided. If you have an extra amp of some kind or a mini-PA and you have the room for it, bring it as well. You might show up somewhere and find that they have absolutely no PA (or a broken one) and thus no way to hear your sweet, sweet voices.

Your gear will be in a cycle of unpack, abuse, pack. Every day. Cords will crud out, batteries will die, drumheads will tear, and strings will break. Take some spares. You know where the good deals are in your hometown, but when you're out and about, you're at the mercy of what each town has to offer. And again, try to get what you can when you're flush with cash in the beginning, instead of spending your food allowance on necessary gear later.

You should also label your cords, cases, and pretty much every piece of equipment you have to make it less likely that someone will walk off with something of yours. You can write your band's name on strips of masking tape, or you can get some colored tape and mark your stuff to make it easier to sort at shows.

Now, the part that techies have trouble with: sizing down the gear. Sit your drummer down and ask him or her, "Do you really need six toms and five cymbals? It's not that you're not a terrific drummer. It's just that . . . well, we'll have to leave someone behind if we take your

Two-Week Tour Packing Profile #3
la foofaraw

sixteen t-shirts →

shades →

laptop →

four shirts →

← two hoodies

sweater

music player

two jackets

four pairs of jeans, four pairs of other pants

hat

→ can be subbed out for skirts *

five pairs of shorts

6 pairs of shoes

or swimsuit

phone

books, journal, puzzles, pens, video games

camera

18 undies

ten bras *

lady stuff *

toothbrush + paste, shampoo, conditioner, hair product + brush, deodorant, shaving stuff, hair dryer, face wash + toner, lotion, soap, makeup *

★ depending on your business, your biznass

Two-Week Tour Packing Profile #3

la foofaraw

continued

two packs of socks

nail clippers

wrinkle removing spray

couple more t-shirts

mouth wash

blanket

shower brush

yoga mat

zines

cotton swabs

And no matter how you pack, don't forget your...

ear plugs

sunscreen

glasses / contacts stuff

phone and other chargers

meds

lip balm

wallet and keys

multi-tool

your copy of PUNK ROCK ETIQUETTE

little sewing kit

music, music, music

towel

sleeping bag

pillow

entire kit." Likewise, having a backup guitar is smart when it comes to broken strings, but don't go crazy. There was a terrible band in eastern New Mexico that once played with eleven guitars on a rack onstage. Guess which string broke during their set. That's right—a bass string. Guess what else. That's right! There was no backup bass. Total dead air for five minutes. So THOSE guys looked like total clowns. (*Note:* Generally bass strings don't break nearly as often as guitar strings do, so don't worry if you don't have a backup bass.)

Merch

An organized merch bin will save you a lot of time if you're in the middle of a consumer feeding frenzy. You'll also know how much of everything you have left. You won't be surprised that you're out of CDs on the ONE NIGHT that fifty people show up and all want to buy your music. If you take supplies to restock (like if you're burning CDs and making your sleeves) and keep track of what you have, you're golden.

If it's taking you three minutes to find a size each time someone wants to buy a shirt, the people in the back of the mass who don't 100 percent want to buy something will change their minds. Fold and roll your shirts into little tubey things and keep them from coming undone

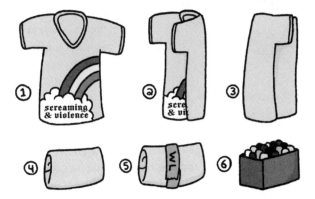

with a piece of masking tape. Then write the size of the shirt on the tape with a marker. So when that boy with the side-swept bangs steps up and asks, "Do you have an extra small?" you can snag one in about two seconds. And the next day at school, he'll be rocking your T-shirt in the cafeteria and thinking about how awesome and professional your band was instead of thinking about how his parents don't understand that he's an ARTIST and he'll NEVER take over the family business. NEVER!

Along with the stuff for sale, try to have something to give out for free. That could be buttons, stickers, trading cards, trinkets, etc.—something that the most penniless of paupers can use to look you up online later. And who knows? Someone might grab a free sticker

from you and put it on their guitar case. A year later, they inherit a big chunk of cash and start a really cool record label. After building some momentum, they contact you and put out your next record. It garners a bunch of attention and good reviews, your shows get bigger and bigger, and then you totally sell out to a cell phone commercial. *Cha-ching!* You're young and rich and hang out with rappers. (Individual results may vary.)

You might also want to have some sort of mailing list. Include spaces for people to put their names, e-mail addresses, and mailing addresses. Put a note at the top of each page PLEADING for legible handwriting—that and a promise that you won't flood them with messages all the time. A mailing list should be used only to announce tours and new records and other things that are actually important.

If you can score one, a battery-powered lamp is a great thing to take along. Illuminating your merch table in a darkened space is guaranteed to increase your sales. Moths to a flame, baby. Moths to a flame.

Food

Rock fuel. You need it. You won't have a kitchen at your disposal twenty-four hours a day, so you'll need to be prepared to fend for yourself out in the wild. Highway convenience stores can't properly sustain you, and spending precious gas money at restaurants all the time might leave you stranded, so packing some essentials can really keep you out of a jam. *Mmmmm. . . jam.*

Make room for a good-sized cooler for some basic staples to keep you alive. Stuff like peanut butter and jelly. Baby carrots! A couple of gallons of water that you can refill as needed. Depending on the season and where you are, you'll have to change out the ice daily or every few days, so make sure everything in the cooler is bagged up all water-proof-like.

Other stuff that's great to pack: crackers, fruit leather, and trail mix. You'll want compact, nutritious stuff that will fill you up. If you don't want to be at the mercy of convenience-store microwaves, take an electric teakettle with you. With it, you can boil water for tea, dehydrated soup, and noodle bowls. Get a car adapter for it and you'll be living large. But keep in mind that it's probably not a good idea to boil water while the car is in motion.

There is one amazing road recipe that really should be used, adapted, and enjoyed by every touring band in the world. That recipe is . . . Shaun Chow. Shaun Chow was developed by Shaun Jones, rock-and-roll drummer, studio engineer, designer, and marketing machine. Shaun Chow stretches the touring budget by providing a nonperishable, abundant, easy-to-prepare food that is very nutritious. It also keeps things moving, if you catch the drift being thrown in your direction. There is no specific recipe, but it starts like this:

Go to the bulk bin at your finer grocery store or health-food store to gather:

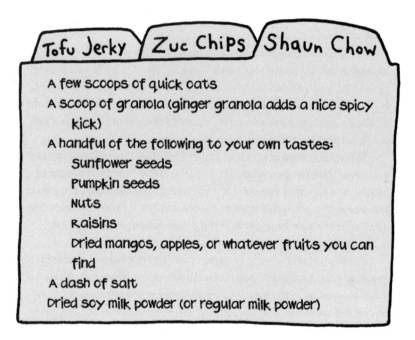

Tofu Jerky | **Zuc Chips** | **Shaun Chow**

A few scoops of quick oats
A scoop of granola (ginger granola adds a nice spicy kick)
A handful of the following to your own tastes:
Sunflower seeds
Pumpkin seeds
Nuts
Raisins
Dried mangos, apples, or whatever fruits you can find
A dash of salt
Dried soy milk powder (or regular milk powder)

Get as much organic stuff as you can. Avoid stuff with refined sugar so you can have sustained energy. If it's not sweet enough, just add more fruit. Mix all of these in a bag. Double bag it to make sure it doesn't get everywhere.

Pack an enameled mug (or titanium or whatever you use for camping) and a spoon. This makes it harder to spill when you eat. To eat, shake the bag, fill up your cup, and pour cold water over it. The water will mix with the powdered milk, and there you have it. This recipe will make about a week's worth of chow.

Maps and Info

Did you pack your maps, directions, and contact information like you were told? DO IT!

Getting It All in There

If you're so inclined, practice getting everything loaded up before the day your tour starts. Then you'll know if you need to rethink some stuff. Otherwise, just pack smart and you'll probably be okay. Load the bigger stuff first and let the little things settle in the spaces and on top. Make sure to leave room so you can see out the back window (it's required by law in some places). Secure everything so that stray equipment won't hit anybody in the back of the head if there's a sudden stop or quick turn. After a couple of days, you'll have figured out the best system for getting it all in okay.

FREEEEEDOM!

It's actually happening. You're packed and loaded, you're all seated comfortably, and you've just left the city limits. You are officially on tour. Adventure, ho!

Traveling

All right, it's time to square away some things. The person driving should be, you know, not terrible at it. If you're taking turns driving, skip the bandmate who tends to wreck cars and get tickets. One or two people can handle all of the driving. It's almost just as important that the person sitting shotgun does his or her job, which is navigating and keeping the driver awake. The kids in the back can sleep or play games or read or count cows or do whatever they want.

Getting along with each other can be a challenge on a long tour. You're spending twenty-four hours a day together, eating, sleeping, and working. And to top it all off, a lot of your time is spent trapped shoulder to shoulder in a little metal box. Take turns picking music in the van. When you're not driving or playing, try to have a little bit of "me" time when you can. Sit outside for a few minutes while everyone else is inside, or find a chair somewhere and relax by yourself. Once you get all huge and have a tour bus, you'll each have a little coffin cabin to relax in. For now, you'll have to take what you can get. If you start hating each other, it will show onstage.

The Law

When you pile a bunch of dirty ne'er-do-wells in a van and start driving across the country, especially in rural areas, you can expect to have a run-in with the Law. Fortunately, if you're not a moron about it, you won't have any problems.

The best way to avoid a bad situation is to not draw attention to yourselves. Drive the speed limit, use your signals, and do all of that other stuff you're supposed to do while driving. Have your registration and insurance up to date, and make sure your license is in good standing if you're behind the wheel. Do not, repeat, do NOT drink and drive. EVER. Do not have anything illegal in your possession or anywhere in the vehicle. Be good boys and girls.

If you get pulled over, be calm and respectful. Have your information ready to give to the officer. When spoken to, use "sir" or "ma'am" (appropriately). Don't make any jokes about guns or drugs—chances are, the officer won't find them funny. Don't lie when asked what you're doing. You're a band on tour. Maybe you're . . . a Christian band on tour. That could be a nice thing to say. This is where a Jesus fish hanging in your rearview mirror might pay off. If you have Mohawks, tattoos, and facial piercings, expect extra scrutiny. If you're asked to step out of the car, you probably want to go ahead and comply.

Now, here's the tricky part: If they ask to search your car, you should know that you don't have to say yes. Fourth Amendment, kid! Unless they have probable cause for a search, they need a warrant. However, probable cause is a very malleable ball of putty. Smells, sights, hey-what's-that-bag, Grateful Dead stickers (though . . . why would you?), etc. can all be "probable cause." Bottom line, you don't want it to get to that point. But if it does, flex your rights if you want . . . but make sure you have time to sit on the side of the road while warrants are obtained. On the other hand, they might not want to mess with it and just let you go. It's a gamble. Oh, and if you're stopped by border patrol, you HAVE to let them search your car if they ask. That's just the way it goes. Again, the importance of keeping your vehicle clean of dirty, dirty sins.

Crossing the border, ESPECIALLY the Canada/U.S. border, is a whole different game. There's this whole worker-competition and preservation-of-culture thing. Canada is afraid of American influence and vice versa. The other concern is taking money out of one economy and spending it another. It makes sense on a grand scale, but you're most likely going to spend any money you make across the border getting back to the other side. However, the Man doesn't understand that. So you'll have to have your chips in order to get across.

If you're planning to take your tour to foreigner-land, you'll need to have proof of citizenship, AKA a passport. It can take a few months to get it after you apply, so plan ahead. The laws change from time to time, so make sure you know what the current requirements are before you take off.

The last thing this here book would EVER, EVER do is tell you to do anything illegal. It's hard to have a going band from prison (unless you're a Scandinavian black metal band). If you get caught lying to an officer at the border, you could get tossed in jail and/or banned from the country you tried to hoodwink your way into. The official and legal way to get across is to get your proper tax paperwork and work visas. You can look up the information on what the sales taxes will be on your merch and get it across that way. Unfortunately, this will cost more money than you can hope to make if you're not a well-known, well-paid band.

A lot of bands have had luck getting across the border with a letter from the venue stating that they were playing a free benefit or fund-raiser show and have nothing to sell. If that's the case, do NOT have any merch in your vehicle. Once upon a time, a band shipped merch across the border to a friend or venue. However, if you pay taxes at the border, you can get a refund of the taxes on the items you don't sell. If you ship your merch, you can't get the shipping costs back.

Depending on what you have, it would probably save you money to just pay the taxes. Come on! Taxes are important! Just think of it this way: A tiny, itty-bitty bit of those taxes will go to fund the arts. Do your part. Also, consider not having your CDs for sale at all. Once upon a time, a band put stickers on their CDs that said, "For promotional use only—not for sale." Ahem.

Again, lying to a border-patrol officer can get you in megatrouble. The oldest trick in the book is saying you're going to a recording studio. Remember how useful the Internet has been to you and your band? Well, guess what? The Man has the Interwebs, too. They can look up your band and see that, whoops, you're not recording at all. You're playing four shows in their country. BUSTED. Wanting to use a bogus band name? Well, not only can they look you up by your band name, but they can look you up individually. So look yourself up. Is your name tied to your band? If so, you could be in double trouble for making them go to all of that effort to unravel your pack of lies. They're used to being lied to, and it is their job to sniff out criminals. Criminals like YOU.

Getting across the border to bring the joy of your music to a new and exciting culture is worth the trouble. You might breeze across, and you might be detailed and interrogated individually for several hours. It is completely up to the discretion of the hardworking men and women at the checkpoint. If anyone in your band has a criminal history, you might have a problem. Again, it depends on who happens to be there that day. In some cases, if you had an arrest without conviction ten years prior, it can keep you from crossing. On the other hand, it might not matter if you were convicted of a crime just a few years ago. Meanwhile, 50 Cent (insert rap sheet pun here), was able to get into Canada and play one of their premiere arenas. The difference? He's a millionaire and you're just a bunch of ruffians. Think he spent all of his money in Canada? Heck, no. He took it HOME. You, however, would be buying gas and food and gas and drinks and gas and records and gas. And gas. Right there in the economy that paid you. O Canada!

No matter how you're doing it, when you get to the border, you will be asked a few questions. Primarily, they want to know what your business is in their country and if you have anything to declare. They might search your vehicle for contraband. That includes weapons, drugs, fruit, etc. Try to cross at nonpeak hours to lessen your wait time a bit. You might be stuck at the checkpoint for hours (it's not unheard of to be there for over seven), so give yourself enough time to get where you're going.

Um . . . once upon a time there was a group of friends on a little road trip. They were in a station wagon and were dressed nicely in name-brand clothing. They had a few days worth of clothing and toiletries. They were going to Canada to shop and see some friends. At the border, they were asked a few questions and had their IDs checked. After the brief search of their vehicle revealed nothing, they were welcomed into Canada. Once there, they arrived at a venue, ROCKED THE PLACE with borrowed equipment, sold a bit of merch that was delivered by a Canuck who had received it in the mail, and made lots of new friends. They made just a little bit of money, and spent most of it at the wide variety of awesome restaurants, record stores, and shops that Canada has to offer. They also shipped the remainder of the merch that was with them in Canada back to the States. With the rest of their money, they filled up their gas tank and headed back to the U.S. of A. With only a few new records to declare, they were back across after a quick drug search. They got back to their equipment and the rest of their stuff, which was waiting for them at a friend's house, and went back on their way. Sweet land of liberty!

Prometheus Delivers the FIRE

Try to show up early in each town so you have ample time to find the venue, meet up with friends, get some food, or just relax for a bit. If you show up five hours early, SURELY you can find something to do other than loiter around in the parking lot. Even the tiniest towns have stuff to do if you make an effort. Car shows, flea markets, bake sales! This is where proper planning in the beginning can pay off. Touring is an adventure. Make it more than playing shows.

When it's time to report to the venue, figure out who's running things and let them know who you are. Get final load-in information and where you fall in the band lineup, as well as any information about the PA or where the free cookies are. Meet the other bands and talk to people.

Also, remember that stage etiquette applies even more on tour than it does at home. You're reppin' your hood! Put on good shows and be friendly, and your tour—and the next—will be more successful. Know that some shows will suck. Fortunately, even moderately well-planned tours should produce two or more amazing shows that can float you through the tough times, both financially and funwise.

The Fall-Through

No matter how well you plan, sometimes a show will fall through at the last minute. Also, you might have tried everything possible and still not been able to book a show somewhere. So what do you do? Take a day off? Or do you roll up your sleeves and ROCK ANYWAY? You've got options.

 If you get to the show and the place is closed, double booked, or not booked (as in someone forgot to write it down), ask anyone who showed up if somebody has a house you can play or if there's a backup venue somewhere.

If you've got a bunch of people who have showed up to see you play but the venue has fallen through and no one has a house you can play, ask around about an old building or bridge or parking lot with an outlet. Give the people what they want! It's your duty!

 Ask around about open mics in town. Yes, they're lame, but you can ask the person emceeing if you can have some sort of extended set. They might give you fifteen to twenty minutes or so to play for tip money, and you can sell a couple of CDs.

 Play on the sidewalk somewhere. Somewhere busy.

. . . Aw, heck. Just take a day off. Relax.

Caaaaash Money

While on tour, your primary income is door money and merch money. If you've planned well and people are showing up, you will be okay. If you have a few off days in a row, you might have to dip into personal money from checking accounts or cash you brought along. There are ways to improve your money from shows, as well as other ways you can generate income while out on the road. Read on, you capitalist pig.

In the basic economic structure, goods and services are exchanged for money or other goods. If you want to sell your merch for delicious cupcakes, that's great! But you'll probably need to sell at least some of your merch for money so you can buy gas. Your prices should be fair and attainable, but some folks just don't have a lot of disposable income. At the risk of coming off all hippie-ish, why not have a sliding scale? For example, price your CD at $6 to $10. Sure, a lot of people will give you six bucks, but you will get some ten-dollar purchases as well. Give your buttons and stickers away for free or for donation. When people of higher means like you, they'll want to support you. If they go the high-dollar route, give them a free button or something.

Don't worry, friends. Tip jars aren't just for bar bands anymore. There's no shame in it at a free show, and at a house show, the hosts will probably pass the hat. If it makes you feel better, write the word "donations" on the bucket. It sounds a little less d-baggy.

Playing in the street goes back to ancient Egypt. Check local laws and decide whether you want to, you know, disturb the peace. Don't set up your amps or anything. Keep it simple and mobile. Singing and playing a guitar in a busy area for a few hours can get you the funds necessary to make it to the next town. Throw in an accordion, toy piano, banjo, or anything else "weird," and the normals will pee themselves to give you money. Playing in the street during the day can also help promote a show that night. Another reason to get to the next town early.

If you make comics or zines, bring them along to sell at shows. Also, hit up local comic book shops and indie/radical/co-op bookstores that carry zines and see about selling some stuff at wholesale rates (consignment doesn't help you when you're on the road). Make some phone calls and be sure that you're not burning up eight dollars in gas to get to a shop that will buy only five dollars worth of zines from you.

Get creative. There are a million ways to get by without resorting to panhandling. You got skills! Use them!

So when you get paid for a show, how do you divide the money? There are a few ways. Some bands put it all in the band fund (for gas and other group expenses like more merch, strings, etc.) and give each member a set daily allowance. Others divide it all up and then each pitch in for gas. A method that seems to work pretty well is to put half in the band fund and split the other half among each member. That way, if you have a really great night, there's a little extra to go around, and your group expenses are taken care of. Should guitar strings and drumsticks come out of the band fund or from the members who need them? On tour, they should probably come out of the band fund. Back in the real world, get your own stuff. But do what you want. If your drummer is breaking heads every night, you'll probably get sick of the band having to pay for them.

Health! Nutrition!

You've GOT to take care of yourself out there. If you get sick, your shows will suck, and everyone will HATE YOU. Okay, now that you're good and scared, maybe you'll take this seriously.

Yes. Pirates are cool. Everyone can agree with that. Being a traveling punk band is a lot like being pirates, and just like your heroes,

you can also get scurvy. Awesome, right? YAARRR!!! Liver spots! Loss of teeth! Bleeding from your wee-wee! Eat a steady diet of beef jerky and corn chips and you just might become a scurvy knave! It's easy to prevent: get that vitamin C. You don't need to bring a barrel of limes with you à la the British Navy. Eat fruits and vegetables every once in a while. If you're staying at a house and have the option of juice or soda, go for the juice. You can still swashbuckle, pillage, and otherwise enjoy the sweet trade. Just do it smartly, ye gentlemen and ladies of fortune.

Being on tour is like having one never-ending weekend. The people you hang out with in each town will be up late getting krunk and rebellious, and they'll want YOU to stay up with them. Just make sure you're not overdoing it. Don't feel bad about skipping out early if you have a long drive the next day. At the very least, the driver should make sure to get enough sleep.

If you sing (or scream), you need to take care of your voice. First off, if you're a singer, you really shouldn't smoke or be around a lot of smoke. You might also try to slow down on the caffeine and alcohol—they're diuretics (they make you pee and dry you out), and you need to hold on to your water (which you should drink lots and lots of). Also, try hot tea (but not too hot, as you can damage your cords that way) in the morning and at night. Again, avoid caffeine if you can—there are teas out there specifically for throat care. Dairy foods and beverages also gunk up your throat. Even if you feel like you're coming down with something, avoid antihistamines if you can, because even though they will dry up the mucus, they'll also dry out your throat. Oh, and some singers take a speaking break from the end of a show until the next morning. Do that, and people will find you mysterious and sexy. Or weird.

In summation, to stay healthy on tour:

o	☐ Eat right
	☐ Drink water
	☐ Breathe air
	☐ Sleep
o	☐ Be nice to your ears

Safety

It's a dangerous world. You should probably just lock yourself inside your room, lit by four televisions, and allow yourself to go slowly insane. NO! Life is for living, so get out there. Just be safe.

When you're out on tour, it's easy to get caught up in the whirlwind of a responsibility-free lifestyle. Don't stop paying attention to your surroundings. A lot of punk venues and houses are in bad neighborhoods. Don't wander off alone at night, and have a phone handy. When you're shacked up for the night, either bring your expensive equipment in or leave it and have someone sleep in the van and protect it (in other words, scream like a maniac and honk the horn if someone tries to break in). If your equipment is in a trailer, park it so the door is blocked by a building or another car that will be there all night.

If you feel totally sketched out by where you are, you always have the option of leaving.

You should also be extremely careful while driving. It's a good idea to make a rule that the person sitting shotgun has to stay awake to keep an eye on the driver. They can also read maps and look out for wild animals.

Someone in your band should have a cell phone. Come on! What year is it?! Access to roadside assistance and emergency contacts is a must. Not to mention the ability to make calls to venues and friends along the way.

EARPLUGS!

Damage to your hearing is permanent. Shows are loud. Take earplugs and wear them. If you're a lo-fi, quiet, shoe-gazey band and you're only playing small house shows on tour, take earplugs anyway. You never know—some obnoxious, loud bands might be booked along with you at some point.

Accommodations

Unless you're getting big fat guarantees—or are Rich Kids—you'll probably be crashing at someone's house most nights. Some outside of the punk community view this as mooching. No, no, no; it's just another branch of the network. You stay with people, and maybe they'll stay with you someday on tour. Hotels often aren't an option, except maybe on occasion if you're doing well financially and need to detox and be quiet for a night.

A lot of the time, you won't know where you'll be sleeping until after a show. You might get an offer on the night. It can get tedious to be constantly looking for a place to stay, so having at least some of your arrangements squared away before you leave for tour can relieve some stress. The person who booked the show might offer some suggestions as well. You might end up at a sickening roach free-for-all beyond your worst nightmares, and you might find yourself in the most balla beach house you've ever seen. On some nights, you might have no alternative but to sleep in your car. It'll be different every night, and that's part of what makes touring exciting.

Be safe!

Don't feel obligated to take your first offer. Think of it as if you're the most popular girl in school, and the big dance is coming up. Should you go with Boogerface Kirkpatrick because he asked first, or should you hold off and see if Johnny Handsome asks? Yeah, you'll probably get a few offers, and if your first seems sketchy or awkward, just say that you're still trying to figure out what's going on and you need to talk to the rest of the band. Then shop around and figure out your best option. Use your judgment! SERIOUSLY! BE SAFE!

When securing a location for the night, be sure that you'll be okay as far as allergies. If your singer is allergic to cats, the last thing you want is for him or her to breathe dander all night.

There's often a direct correlation between how you look and act and where you'll end up. If you're a bunch of gutter punks, you'll probably end up on the . . . lower end of the hygiene spectrum of housing most of the time. And that's okay if that's what you're comfortable with. Likewise, if you're a bunch of clean sweethearts, you might get taken home to Mommy. Before you stay with someone who lives with his or her parents, make sure it's cool. If it has to more or less be a secret, or if they're not usually okay with things like that, look elsewhere. Or you might luck out and be greeted at the door by Mom and Dad and offers of food and clean sheets. In the morning, you'll relive the glory days of music over pancakes and fresh fruit. Ah, *la vita è bella!*

Roadmance

It's a scientific FACT that being on tour makes little hormone bubbles fizzle in your brain that make you want to get your smooch on. Yes, that is the scientific way to put it. It's the result of receiving acclaim and the freedom to basically do what the heck you want in a consequence-free environment. Ooh, baby. You'll be around a lot of people, and you'll probably meet at least one person along the way who you think is cute. Roadmance is in the air. So, should you go for it?

Don't be a jerk. If you're in a relationship back home, do you REALLY want to be a cheater? You're in a different zip code, but it still counts, despite what your cool uncle says. Your bandmates will know, and the friends of the person you're cheating with will know. It could get back to your boy/girlfriend, and not only that, it's just . . . wrong!

If you're in a bit of a rocky relationship to begin with, and you don't think it will last much longer anyway, maybe you should get out of it before the tour. But don't be obvious about it. Don't break it off in the driveway with the engine running right before you leave. Be a little bit more sneaky.

It's hard to know where you stand in your relationship sometimes, but try your best to figure that out before you go out in the wide world. You never know. You might be totally good and faithful and not even LOOK at anyone else while on tour for a month, and then come back to town only to get immediately dumped. Um . . . that's just . . . hypothetical.

Don't be a creep! If you're in your midtwenties, you have no business getting involved with a sixteen-year-old. GRODY. And don't be a trollop. If you go around making out with people every time you put the van in park, you will get a bad rep. Your band will get a bad rep. Again, you are not Def Leppard. Please quit trying.

But if you're available and legal and you meet someone nice, let the roadmance commence.

Post-Tour Trauma

It's over. The adventure has ended (for now), and you're back to your real life. You've got a bag full of disgusting, dirty clothes, and you feel like hammered dog poo. The abrupt lifestyle change of coming home from tour can be downright depressing, even if you were ready to be home. So how can you conquer the post-tour trauma? Here are some suggestions:

If you have a job to get back to, it would be best if you didn't have to start again immediately. Having at least a day off before donning your apron, name tag, or silly hat would be good for you.

Take a long shower or bath.

 Do your laundry. Like, REALLY do it. With dryer sheets and all of that other nice stuff you normally skimp on.

 Eat at your favorite restaurant. If you're broke, maybe you've got a friend who missed you and would love to take you out. Get an appetizer and dessert, too.

 Ride a bike or go hiking. Anything where you're moving around without really heading somewhere.

 Go to a show. Yes, you've been to shows every night for a while, but going to a show where you don't have to DO anything can be refreshing. It can also re-jazz you about playing music.

Play with a puppy. If that doesn't cheer you up, there's no hope.

A lot of bands split up after touring. If things went well and everyone got along, don't take too long of a break before getting back together to practice and play shows. If a month or more passes without the band getting together, the momentum might die, and with it, your band. What would the world do without your music? Please. Think of the children.

Going on tour is the pinnacle of being in a band. Do it, even if you can only get away for long weekends. Traveling, meeting people, and exploring is one of the most rewarding things a person can do. So get your band together and go! Go!

Even if playing in a band doesn't become your lifelong career, or even something that you do to pay the bills for a while, it will be a part of your time on this giant tour van called Earth that you can be proud of. You contributed to (sub)culture! You got involved! Congratulations! When you're old and gray and the Great Space Wars have ended, gather the children and apes together in the ruins of a once-great city and pass down the knowledge of the Time Before. A time when adventurers banded together, looked life square in the eyeballs, and rocked.

Now get started!

GLOSSARY

arena rock: Music performed in giant stadiums with huge production values.

balla: You know, like, rich and flashy.

booker: Sometimes interchangeable with "promoter." The person who books a show.

cassingle: A cassette single. One of the most horribly awesome or awesomely horrible things the music industry ever came up with.

chorus: The sound effect of making one thing sound like a lot of things.

cred: As in credibility.

DIY: Umm... Do It Yourself. Whether you're building a bird house on your own or putting out your band's record, it's action, approach, and attitude.

door: The money that is collected from people paying to see the show.

fills: Little bits of shredding done on an instrument to add hot, hot flavor to music. Flibbity-bippity-POW!

flanger: Generates the sound effect of "beeeeeorps" created by teeny weeny time delays. Also, the sound effect of repetition/echo created by looping audio input.

front man: The main member of the band. The guy who's in the middle of all the photos, usually pointing at the camera like he's in Menudo or something. Don't say this! It's LAME!

greasel: Fuel made from cooking oils that you filter right in the car (converting to biodiesel). Look into this stuff.

guarantee: A promised amount of money you'll receive for playing a show. No matter how many people show up, if you have a guarantee, you're golden. Maybe.

headlining: An ancient term for the big shot on the show bill. Do not use this term.

jongleurs: Wandering entertainers in medieval France and England. Oh! You just got some knowledge dropped on you!

krunk: Are you completely out of touch? Go to the mall or watch TV or something.

liner notes: The information on a music release's album insert and/or case.

load-in: When and where you're supposed to put your gear.

lo-fi: Short for "low fidelity." A general term used for music produced at less than stellar quality. Can be redeeming and comfy . . . or crummy sounding.

merch: Short for "merchandise." The band-related stuff you sell to buy microwave burritos and 64-ounce soft drinks. (Gross!)

modge podge: Craft glue for collage, etc. that is good for painting on screens.

monitors: The speakers on stage that face the band so they can hear themselves. You sound incredible.

nomad sandwich: The best way to line up a show for a touring band. A local band before the touring band(s), and a local band after. That way, people are more likely to stick around.

PA: That thing. That all of the microphones are plugged into. That the speakers go out of.

pop filter: Take a piece of wire (such as from a metal clothes hanger) and make it into a loop. Stretch some pantyhose over it and attach it a few inches in front of your microphone when you're recording. It'll help reduce hard "PPP!" and "TTT!" sounds when you sing.

post-tour trauma: The depression that comes when a tour ends. Quick! Book another one!

press(ed): As in "getting a record pressed." For vinyl, the music is physically smooshed into the grooves. It's a stinking miracle of science, people.

reverb: The sound effect of a big empty room. Ooooooooooh. Dreamy.

rider: When you're a big shot, you get to write a list of things you want the venue to provide in addition to payment. Deli trays, freshly-squeezed juices, clean white towels, British-imported Skittles with the green ones removed, etc.

roadie: No, no. Say "tour support." A pal who goes with your band on the road to work the merch table, help carry stuff, etc . . . but mostly just hang out because the sandwich shop where they worked fired them for giving away too much food, and now they totally have free time.

roadmance: Sweet, sweet stranger. I am but a traveling music maker. I shall be gone tomorrow, but tonight, oh, tonight, we shall make out.

scene: Your town, your people, heritage. Often a source of pride more blind and defensive than that of the typical überpatriot. "Don't go bringing that crap into MY scene!"

synthy: Laden with synthesizers. Awesome.

sound engineer: A tech nerd who runs the PA at shows or the gear at a recording studio.

track: A recorded part of music. If you're recording on a multi-track recorder, each part will go on a different track. Savvy?

white-towel treatment: Arena rock standard. (See rider.)

RESOURCES

For further information, check out the following:

Legal stuff

www.copyright.gov: The Library of Congress's Web site that tells you everything you need to know about copyright law. Drown, drown in a sea of legalese.

www.ascap.com / www.bmi.com: If you want to leap into the whole performing-rights-organization abyss, these are the sites of the two biggest.

www.cbp.gov: U.S. Customs and Border Protection. Fill your brainsack with the knowledge on this site to avoid a hassle at the border.

Printing (record/cd sleeves, posters, etc.)

www.pinballpublishing.com / www.1984printing.com: Two of many great places to get super-quality printing for posters, cd/record sleeves, etc. for which Momma Earth will thank you.

More more MORE stuff

www.punkrocketiquette.com: Supplemental information, tour stories, resources for booking, and other totally aces stuff.

ACKNOWLEDGMENTS

(info supply, check-ins, back pats, snacks)

Jessica Wolkoff
Meghan Murphy
Kyle Sowash
Rhonda Turnbough
Al Fair
Jennifer Perkins
Linnea Toney
Cherie Weaver
Brian Flores

CONTRIBUTIONS BY

Michael Mayer
Shaun Jones

DIY music time line

2,200,000 BCE Oog and Ik bang stones together for their tribe, thus inventing indie rock.

360 BCE - The members of Salamis know they're doing the right thing when Plato rants about new music "breakin established forms blah blah blah.

2936 BCE - Forgoing connections to the royal household, Egypt's Akhet tours the festival circuit, playing and selling the first merch-small paintings of the group on sheets of papyrus.

1286 CE - By drawi inspiration from Gre chant and hinting sacred themes, Fran Bornelh is able to p at monasteries and r the white linen treat

INDEX

4 – Ideological
erences split up
den Hill when
members say
want a revolution
two head to
ian Territory.

1950s – Indie labels pop up when majors prove to be a bunch of squares, daddy-o.

1990s, 2000s – affordable home recording equipment and the internet spawns ONE BILLION BANDS.

883 – Former members of Rattlesnake Pass join the Buffalo Bill Wild West Show and lose half of their original fanbase.

1970s, 1980s – Some stuff happens. Bands and stuff. Video kills radio star ; home taping kills music.

2146 – All systems of government fail; anarchy in the UK actualized. Guitars rebuilt as battle axes.

P

Packing: equipment, 102–103

Performing rights organizations, 35–36

Pinball Publishing, 32

Pins, 49. *See also* Promoting

Plaid pants, 13

Playing cards, 50

Poor kid: as personality type, 8

Poor kid/delinquent: as personality type, 10

Portal sites, 36

Posse: forming, 5

Post-tour trauma, 124–126

Posters. *See also* Promoting: screen printing for, 48

Practicing: before recording, 26; finding space for, 16–17

Profile sites, 36–37

Promoting: your shows, 90

Punk hangouts, 86

R

Recording: break ups and, 28; budget and, 27; space for, 23

Rich kid: as personality type, 8

Rich kid/delinquent: as personality type, 10

Roadies, 94

Roadmance, 122–123

Rock star: as personality type, 7

Rock star/delinquent: as personality type, 10

Royalties, 35–36

S

Screen printing: instructions for, 42–47

Set: things to do during, 56

Setup: before performances, 54–55

Shows. *See also* Tours: booking, 16

Sleeves: artwork for, 34

Social networking, 36

Stage: etiquette on, 53

Studios, 24–28

T

T-shirts: purchasing, 48

Tattoos, 13

Techie: as personality type, 7

Tortured poet/poor kid: as personality type, 10

Tortured poet/rock star: as personality type, 10

Tour support, 88. *See also* Tours

Tours: booking, 82–89; packing